His Way

By David Knight

An Everyday Plan for Following Jesus

Nihil Obstat:
    Rev. Lawrence Landini, O.F.M.
    Rev. John J. Jennings
Imprimi Potest:
    Rev. Andrew Fox, O.F.M.
    Provincial
Imprimatur:
    +Daniel E. Pilarczyk, V.G.
    Archdiocese of Cincinnati
    April 1, 1977

The *Nihil Obstat* and *Imprimatur* are a declaration that a book or
pamphlet is considered to be free from doctrinal or moral error. It
is not implied that those who have granted the *Nihil Obstat* and
Imprimatur agree with the contents, opinions or statements
expressed.

Illustrations by Mary Beth Froehlich
Cover design by Kieran Quinn
(former SBN 0-912228-39-3)

Reprinted 1997

ISBN 0-942971-24-8

1310 Dellwood Avenue
Memphis TN 38127
901-357-6662
(FAX 901-353-3783)

The royalties that would normally be paid to the author or the House of the Lord community are being given to the poor.

Contents

Contents

PREFACE

It will be 15 years on December 25 of this year since the Holy Father, Pope John XXIII, issued the convocation of the Second Vatican Ecumenical Council for 1962. The text stated: "Today the Church is witnessing a crisis underway within society. While humanity is on the edge of a new era, tasks of immense gravity and amplitude await the Church, as in the most tragic periods of its history. It is a question, in fact, of bringing the modern world into contact with the vivifying and perennial energies of the gospel, a world which exalts itself with its conquests in the technical and scientific fields but which brings also the consequences of a temporal order which some have wished to reorganize excluding God. This is why modern society is earmarked by a great material progress to which there is not a corresponding advance in the moral field."

Pope John discerned the signs of the time and he moved to provide meaning to life where there was none, hope where there was despair. And now we too see the signs of the renewing Church as it continues on the path of that new Pentecost.

A sign of the time is the development of our recognition of the essential necessity of a prayer life. The stress of renewal revealed a lack of depth and sometimes no reality to the prayer life of our people. The Spirit of God prompted the awareness of this insufficiency and encouraged us to know that Jesus was the center of that life, that to put on Jesus was not a mere catch phrase, but the core of our encounter with him.

One awareness leads to another as the Spirit continues us along the pilgrim path. To put on Jesus causes reflection on the culture which had been our clothing. The more we encountered Jesus, the less well suited we became for the civil religion.

Awareness of Jesus causes us to embrace our brothers and sisters with a new love, the same love he bears them. And so our community grows into the Body of Christ.

Father David Knight helps us along our way as his insights clarify the areas of gray. He sweeps away the fogginess of some of the ideas which we hold so firmly simply because they have been with us a long time.

He leads us through prayer to the unity of the Eucharist where we praise God for his loving work. He leads us through the unity of this community to the renewal of the society in which we pray.

+Carroll T. Dozier
Bishop of Memphis

I want to thank Sister Agnes Stretz of the Order of St. Clare who typed this manuscript as fast as I could get it written and whose enthusiasm for the project had a great deal to do with its completion. I also owe deep gratitude to the members of my community here at the House of the Lord. Some worked with me as a team on a Lent-long tour of parish missions in Mississippi, Arkansas and Alabama where the ideas in this book took shape. And all cooperated to leave me free, inspired and encouraged to write this book. Without the example of their own radical way of religious life I would never have had the courage to say these things to lay persons.

What to Look for in This Book
INTRODUCTION: *Of Eggs and Caviar*

As soon as you finish writing a book, you start criticizing it. My own criticism of this book is that it may give the impression at times that only big things are important. I use phrases like "prophetic witness" and "Christian reformation of society," for example, that make Christianity sound like something that has to be on the front page before it is news at all.

But this book isn't about the reform of society. It is about knowing Jesus Christ. That is all. Those who know Jesus deeply will be able to know and help each other a little more—maybe a great deal more than we imagine.

What, after all, is the "reformation of society" if it is not helping people feel a little better about themselves and come a little closer to what they are called to be in grace? *Society* is a pretty abstract, faraway word. But the husband or wife next to you in bed, the children who make you laugh and cry (or curse), the man or woman close to you at work, or the person you buy a newspaper from—these are "society" for you, your *real* society.

If you manage to "be Christ" to those around you, I imagine Christ will also be able to work through you for those big, important things in life. Provided you know they are part of the challenge of being a Christian.

What do I, as a priest, know about "lay spirituality"? What do you expect me to know?

I certainly don't know how you, as a layperson, should lead your life. I have no concrete suggestions to make on how to raise the kids, or how to resolve the last problem that came up in your marriage. I don't even know how you ought to vote.

But that's not lay spirituality. Lay spirituality doesn't tell you *what to do*; it tells you *how to live* so that *God himself can show you what to do.*

I can't teach; I can only point. Jesus is the Teacher, and you are just as much his disciple as I am. All this book intends to do is point out *where* Jesus can be looked for in your life and *how* you can clarify and expand your relationship with him.

It offers a "complete" explanation of lay spirituality in the sense that it deals with all three dimensions of human existence: our vertical relationship with God, our horizontal relationship with others, and our in-depth relationship with our own choosing self. It isn't just a book on the interior life, for example, or on the apostolate. It doesn't present one slice or another, but the whole, round cake.

It is also a simple book, and short enough to handle. I don't try to identify and develop every virtue and exercise of the spiritual life. Everything revolves around three basic realities: *prayer, conversion of life* and *community*. If you can handle these, they'll take you to everything else.

Finally, this is the only book I know of (which may just reveal my ignorance) which does justice to the unique, proper, distinct characteristic of *lay* spirituality as such. The spirituality of the layperson should not be modeled on the spirituality of religious orders, no matter how enlightening the charisms of the great religious founders might be. It is very helpful to belong to a Third Order or to a religious association inspired by the spirituality of St. Francis, St. Benedict, St. Dominic, St. Ignatius Loyola, St. Francis de Sales, St. John Baptist de la Salle or one of the other founders. But such associations can only supplement and encourage the true, the essential spirituality of the layperson as such. And this spirituality exists, not in virtue of some association with a religious order, but *by the very fact of being a layperson in this world*.

Vatican II has focused our attention on lay Christians' *secularity* — on their unique characteristic of being involved "in each and in all of the secular professions and occupations. . .in the ordinary circumstances of family and social life, from which the very web of their existence is woven" (*Constitution on the Church*, 31). It is this very involvement with the world which is the foundation of lay spirituality.

Booker T. Washington tells of a ship becalmed off the South American coast when sails were still more common than steam. Crew members were starting to die of thirst when a steamship hove in sight. "Send us water," they signaled. The steamship signaled back, "Send down your bucket where you are."

The sailing ship flagged back, "It is fresh water we need; send us drinking water." Still the steamship signaled back, "Send down your bucket where you are."

When the crew of the sailing vessel finally did lower their bucket into the ocean, it came up filled with fresh, not salt water. The fresh water of the Amazon River is carried 50 miles out to sea when it pours out of its mouth on the coast of Brazil—or so the story goes.

Whether the Amazon really does this, I don't know. But the key line of the story could serve as the guiding principle of lay spirituality: "Send down your bucket where you are."

For a model of lay spirituality we can do no better than to look first at Mary, the Mother of Jesus. She was a layperson: a wife and a mother. She lived her whole life in what the Vatican Council describes as the characteristic situation of the layperson: in the "ordinary circumstances of family and social life," and it was from these that the "very web of her existence was woven." We find her in the Gospels searching for a runaway boy, trying to get her son to come home for dinner, procuring barrels full of wine for a wedding feast! And all of this time she is mirroring for us the attitude we should have toward things, toward people, toward her son, who is the Son of God.

We are told in the Gospels of Jesus going "up the mountain to pray." We never hear of Mary doing this. But she prayed all the same, if never on a mountain top. It was characteristic of her life that, whenever God spoke to her—through his word or through the events in her life—Mary "treasured all these things and reflected on them in her heart" (Lk 2:19).

We know she did pray: She prayed over what God was saying to her through her life; and the results of her prayer appeared in her day-to-day interaction with people, with things, with her environment.

The test of lay spirituality is not the devotion a person experiences in church, but the reflection of Christ's attitudes and values in his life—at home, at work and at play.

I am ordained a priest. I can transform bread and wine. But the first priesthood I knew—and didn't recognize at the time—was the priesthood of my mother: the "priesthood of the faithful." Everything she saw was transformed by the vision of her faith. Everything she touched was in some way lifted up to God.

I found the beginnings of a diary after her death. She had started to write it on her honeymoon and had made only one entry since, when my oldest brother was born. What she wrote on her honeymoon was:

> 1926, May 8, Havana: I always have a feeling of sadness when travelling—a feeling that life holds so much more than I can ever grasp. . . .

> I am going to grow old before my time, because I have always thought married people were old. All I can think of now is my fast-fading youth and the time when memories will have to take the place of ideals.

> That is why I cannot understand why all elderly people do not innately believe in a hereafter. How can anyone end life with a full feeling of accomplishment, and wouldn't the belief in heaven be more welcome than despair?

> Now, heaven is not my immediate ideal, for I cannot lose the feeling that somewhere in life is beauty that I must someday lay my hands on and have for my own.

She was prophetic. It was life that she laid her hands on. And through her "laying on of hands" everything she touched was transformed.

A close friend of mine, a priest, went to see her once when she was living in Paris. He had been working late, was tired, had gone to a movie, and on his way home passed by her apartment.

"I knew she would be up," he told me. "So I just went in. She was having a party. I told her I was tired, had a headache, and would just like to eat a couple of eggs and drink a glass of wine."

"The only eggs we have are caviar," she answered, "and the only wine we have is champagne. Will that do?"

Many years later I read in spiritual books about "finding God in all things." But if I have learned to find God in things and in people at all, I believe I learned it from my mother's approach to life.

Now I have embraced a life of poverty, celibacy and obedience—the religious vows. Not my mother's style of life at all.

Yet it is a way of life she understood, and prepared me for. I hear her saying still, with a different shade of meaning than before: "All the eggs you have are caviar. All the wine you drink is champagne."

When you get right down to it, isn't the marriage feast of Cana what it's really all about?

What Does It Mean to Be a Christian Today?

CHAPTER ONE: *A Very Chummy Mummy*

A friend told me his teenage son had stopped going to Mass. I asked the boy, "Have you left the Church?"

"No, I still believe in the Church. I pray every day. I just don't go to Mass."

"Why not?"

"Well, all they ever talk about is money and drugs. I don't have any money, and I don't take drugs, so why should I go to Mass?"

He thought a minute and added: "Besides, the church is a mausoleum."

Is the "Good News" Really News?

If we are the Church of the Good News, it doesn't sound like it. Let's be honest with ourselves: Is Christianity *news* or not? Do people come to church expecting to hear something they haven't heard before? To experience something they haven't experienced before? Do Christians meet together like marchers in the woods, trying to decide on a course to follow, a direction to take? Or do they file into church like passengers into a subway car, to sit down and endure it while the conductor takes them over the same old route again?

The laity may complain that priests are not inspiring. But priests complain that their ministry is shaped by what the laity asks of them. And what does the laity ask?

A pastor I know made a study once of everything he was asked to do over the course of a week. In a typical day he counted 17 requests that dealt with personnel management (hearing complaints about a teacher, sorting out a fight between the head of the cemetery committee and the man who mowed the grass); 10 with maintenance; five with finances; and one request for confession.

"When people come to see me for advice," he said, "they want to know how to stop their husbands from drinking, how to get their kids to obey them. I am not married, and have never raised kids. I'm not a marriage counselor. There is only one thing I feel I really have to offer."

"And what is that?" I asked him.

"I can teach them how to let Jesus Christ be a real part of their lives. I can teach them how to pray together over the Scripture, for example. That I can do, but that they are not always ready to hear."

And those who are ready to hear it too often do not find a priest prepared to talk about it.

Let's face it: The person of Jesus Christ does not have the place in our lives he ought to have. And this is reason enough to ask just how authentically Christian our Christianity is. Could it be that we have not yet really understood what it is to be a Christian?

If that statement sounds extreme, let us ask for a moment what non-Christian (and-Judaic) religion is. What, in other words, is good, "natural" religion—the religion of those who worship God as best they know how, but do not have the revelation of the Scriptures to go by?

I was a missionary in Africa for three years. In my part of Africa (southern Chad) I would go anywhere by myself alone at night, unarmed, and fear no man. One violent murder occurred in my territory during the three years I was there, and that was the first in about 25 years—the only one most people could remember. Pilfering was fairly common (since the arrival of the white man and the introduction of his ways), but armed robbery was unheard of and break-ins practically nonexistent. Standards of sexual morality were easily as high as in this country and probably much, much higher. In short, the non-Christian Africans I dealt with kept the Ten Commandments better than American Christians seem to keep them.

Their society was simpler, of course. They didn't have to cope with many of the temptations we have created for ourselves. But the point is, these people whom we call "pagans" knew what was right and wrong, and kept to it as well as we do— and they didn't have to be Christians to do this.

What about church? Did they worship God?

They worshiped God as they knew him. And they were more faithful to their rituals and sacrifices than most Christians seem to be to ours. A Gallup poll in November, 1975, showed six out of 10 Americans not attending church or synagogue in a given week; 18 million of these are Catholics.

Are we saying that paganism is superior to Christianity? No, there are many reasons to explain the facts above: simpler society, moral pressures in a closely-knit tribe, superstitious fears, etc. But if Christianity is nothing more than a moral code and a way of paying worship to God, the best it can claim to be is another "natural" religion—what we might call, in somewhat stronger language, an "orthodox paganism."

Code and Cult

Pagan—or natural—religion is basically a religion of *code* and *cult*. People are born into this world, realize that someone else created it before they got here, and ask about the ground rules. They want to know what is right and wrong. This is the first element of natural religion, or of any religion: a *moral code*.

And then, recognizing the fact that everything they enjoy in the world, including their own lives, comes from Someone Else, a Creator, people realize that they should be expressing some acknowledgment of this Power, some appreciation of what it is, some gratitude and respect. And so a *cult* is born: a ritual, a ceremony, a way of paying worship. This is the second element that all religions have in common.

The American Indians in the Northwest never cut into a slain animal until they first sliced off a tiny piece and held it up to heaven in recognition of God. This is cult.

If the moral code of a pagan community is a good one; that is, if it does in fact correspond to right and wrong as God intended man to see these, then the religion of that community is, morally speaking, *good* paganism. (A country like the United States, for example, that accepts the murder, by sterilized hands, of close to one million babies a year through abortion reveals a moral sense that is *bad* paganism. Most natural, unsophisticated pagans would shudder at what we do.)

Likewise, if the cultic ceremonies through which a pagan community expresses its knowledge and recognition of God are in any way appropriate to the dignity and nature of God, if they do illumine rather than obscure the face of God, then the pagan cult is a good one. It may not express, as the Mass does, the divinely revealed truth of God's nature and relationship with man; but if it teaches man something true about himself and God, and expresses something authentic about their relationship, it is a good pagan cult.

Let us ask, quite frankly, whether Christianity is more than this, more than a simple religion of code and cult, for many, many people whom we recognize as Christians. The fact that our moral code may be *right*—as far as it goes in any given age or culture—does not alter the fact. A religion with just the "right" (even a "revealed") moral code, if it has nothing more than this to offer, is not essentially different from any other natural religion. It is still just paganism. It may be an "orthodox" paganism, but it is paganism all the same.

And the same is true of our cult. The fact that Catholics, for example, have the right cult—one which expresses, and even makes present, the true mystery of God's redemptive dealing with man— does not mean a whole lot unless those present at Mass *understand* what is being said and done and *respond* to it in their lives.

We Christians know that Jesus died to redeem us, and we celebrate this reality at Mass. But do we really understand what it means to be "redeemed"— in terms of *living* here and now? And do we know what we are *saying*, and committing ourselves to, when we "celebrate" that fact in the Mass?

The Meaning of Redemption

Our redemption is not just a fact of history that we happen to know about and the pagans don't. There is more to believing in redemption than just going about with a sigh of relief that the "gates of heaven" are now opened and things will be different for us when we die.

Redemption makes things different right now. Our Lord's death on the cross did not just affect the "gates of heaven," or change the Father's attitude toward us. It did something very profound *to us*.

Christ died so that *we* might change, interiorly, in the very core and reality of our being. It is this that we celebrate at Mass. We celebrate what we *are*, what we have *become* by the grace of Christ, and what we are *called to be* in our lives here, on this earth, as living members of his Body.

On Calvary it was not just our sins that were "washed away"; it was *we who died* in Christ in order to rise again in him and live on an entirely new level of human existence. Because we are redeemed, we are now called, and able, to *think* as men have never thought before; to *evaluate* things in this world in a way that overturns all previous standards of judgment; to *act* in ways that are as far beyond what we usually understand by "morality" as the thoughts and ways of God are beyond the thoughts and ways of men.

> For my thoughts are not your thoughts,
>   nor are your ways my ways, says the Lord.
> As high as the heavens are above the earth,

> so high are my ways above your ways
> and my thoughts above your thoughts.
> (Is 55:8-9)

But all of this distance between God and man has been overcome through the redemption that is ours in Jesus Christ. Because we have *died* in him, we have *risen* in him—already—to lead a new life. And this life, which we call the life of grace, is to *share in Christ's life*—that is, in his thinking, his choosing, his appreciating, his knowing and loving and suffering and rejoicing here on this earth—right here and now, until he comes again and we share his life and his joy fully and forever in heaven.

If Christians really expressed themselves, knowingly and consciously, through the gestures of the Mass, every Mass would be a profound act of total commitment to God to live in an entirely new way. Imagine what it would be if every person at Mass deeply and consciously expressed the sincere offering of his whole self to God to be transformed, with the bread and the wine, into a perfectly responsive member of the Body of Christ, dying and rising in him to live a new kind of life, a life according to the attitudes and values, the mind and the heart of Christ himself?

The Image We Project

This would be Christianity. But is this what every Catholic comes to Mass for? The same pastor I quote above says his congregation gives a general impression (which he knew was not fair to the deeper reality of their hearts) of coming to Mass for two things: to be exhorted by the priest to keep the moral code which they already accepted and understood, and to "fulfill their obligation" of paying Sunday worship to God.

"My people are sincere people," he said. "They really want me to persuade them to be more patient with their children, more faithful to their wives, more truthful in their speech. But they are not coming across—clearly, at least—as a *Christian* people, because the last thing they seem to want is for me to push out the frontiers of their moral consciousness. Many of them react as if they do not really want to know what Christ taught, if what he taught is going to ask any more of them than what they learned in grade school.

"And I keep asking myself if they really want to know what the Mass is all about. Some act as if getting out of the parking lot in 50 minutes was the important thing. And within that time they don't want to be roused into thought by any changes in the liturgy. They just want the familiar routine. It almost makes you believe any cult would do for them, so long as they were used to it.

"Once I preached a real strong sermon on sexual morality. The parents followed me back into the sacristy, they were so happy. They do not want their daughters getting pregnant. But if I preach a sermon even half that strong on social justice, or on racial integration, a lot of them act like they'd love to lynch me after Mass."

A congregation that wants to be Christian says to

the pastor, "You make it clear to us that Jesus thought this way or that way, that he would want us to act as you propose, and we will do it." They want to accept—to constantly "convert" to—the mind and heart of Christ, to adopt his attitudes and values. But a congregation comes across as pagan when their basic stance appears to be, "We don't want to hear about it; we know what we are used to, and we don't want to change anything." Such a congregation seems uninterested in entering more deeply into a personal understanding of the mind and heart of Christ, into personal communion with him.

We all need to ask ourselves what type of Christians we are. Not that there are any neat "either-or" categories that real persons fit snugly into. But if we are honest with ourselves we can recognize what attitude predominates in our heart. Is our religion essentially a matter of *morality* and *worship* (doing the right thing in order to get to heaven), a "code and cult" Christianity? Or is it primarily a search for *communion* with the mind and heart of Christ?

Do We Ask the Hard Questions?

People living the "code and cult" reduction of Christianity don't usually ask the questions that would put their whole lives under the light of Christ. They tend to settle for the more obvious moral laws—as learned in the catechism during grade school, or as understood and interpreted by the people around them.

Such people look upon the Ten Commandments

as safe-channel markers. Anyone who has not crossed their clear and obvious line is on the right path out of harm's way. They do not want to sail by a compass, such as the Scriptures or the example of Christ; they don't look beyond their channel; and they don't look up at the stars. They just want to be "kept in line" by the laws; they are not interested in orienting themselves toward a deeper understanding of the Lawgiver, so that the divine attitudes and values which inspired the law will become the very law, the interior compass, of their own hearts.

In other words, they want their consciences left alone. They think that asking questions will narrow their channel, not broaden their horizons. Or they fear that if they think beyond their channel, the challenge will be too much for them.

This leads to a "morality" that leaves most of life's decisions outside of its area of interest. "Religion" is a searchlight that shines on a rather narrow track; what goes on outside of that track is not illumined by religion at all.

When I was in theology we took a course on justice. It was complicated, because so much depends on the laws and business practices of the country. For example, the professor told us that in France, where I was studying, everyone cheats 33 - 1/3 per cent on his income tax. For the French, it's practically a national custom. And so, he told us, if someone comes to confession and says he is cheating 23 - 1/3 per cent on his income tax, you tell him he has another 10 per cent to go!

There were more serious examples, of course, involving business ethics and all kinds of delicately balanced compromises. At the end of the course the professor guessed, quite rightly, that we weren't very confident about going out and handling these difficult moral questions in the confessional. I will never forget the way he reassured us: "Don't worry," he said, *"They will never come up in confession!"*

After 16 years of priesthood, I'm afraid he called it just about right.

The fault does not all lie with the laity. Priests, too, hesitate to bring up the "hard questions" in sermons. It is easier to talk about what everyone already accepts than to try to push forward the frontiers of conscience. A priest in campus ministry at a state university in Illinois shared with me a revealing story told him by a student who had been stationed on an aircraft carrier off the coast of North Vietnam during the war.

"Every day," he said, "we were sending planes to bomb Vietnam. But when the chaplain got up to preach on Sunday, all he ever talked about was how bad it would be for us to go to houses of prostitution—as if we were going to swim off the ship and take a weekend in Hanoi!

"But when I got back to this country, here on this campus with all the beautiful girls walking around and temptation everywhere, what does the chaplain preach about? Pacifism, and the evil of dropping bombs on Vietnam!"

George Gallup discovered in the poll cited earlier
that "roughly three out of four of the public do
not consciously connect religion with their judgments of right or wrong." I am sure that Catholics
connect religion with things like sexual morality,
for example, and murder. But they are not *making
judgments* about these things; they were taught
what was right and wrong in these areas years ago.
If something new comes up—something they do
have to make a judgment about—then Gallup's poll
is probably valid for them, too.

A surprising number of Catholics do not let the
Church's teaching on abortion affect their judgment about this variety of murder—because it is
new, surgical, and the law of our culture has made
it socially acceptable. In a poll conducted by
Father Andrew Greeley in 1974, 70 per cent of the
Catholics polled agreed that legal abortions should
be available for married women who do not want
more children.

In the area of sexual morality (which I point out
because it is popularly believed that here, at least,
the Church has taken a hard line with Catholics),
religion does not seem to have much effect on such
an ordinary thing as modesty, or the way people
dress. It is a fact of life in our times, I believe, although we don't like to admit it, that the average
woman, especially if she is not yet married, is going
to wear just about anything that New York decides
she shall wear . No one pretends that the clothes
one sees today contribute very much to proclaiming the Christian image of woman—or even a very
human image of woman, for that matter. But appar-

ently very few people consider the expression of one's self-image through clothes to be a religious value.

If we move into the more complicated issues of politics, social justice, racial integration, business ethics and war, it is even more apparent that religion has very little, if anything, to do with the moral judgments most people make. According to a *Newsweek* survey (Oct. 4, 1971), what determines a Catholic's attitudes toward real issues in this world, and toward whatever the Church might have to say about them, is not so much his religion as "his income, education, and where he floats in America's still bubbling melting pot."

With regard to simple, black-and-white violations of the Ten Commandments, the Catholic lets the Church judge him; but when it comes to business, politics and everything else men really argue about in this world, he judges the Church. And usually he judges the Church by the standards—and prejudices— of his peer group: his friends, fellow-students, business associates, social milieu.

Civil Religion

What this adds up to is "ethical paganism": a religion of code and cult whose moral code is really determined, not by the revelation of God speaking through the Scriptures, but by the attitudes and values of the society one lives in and the people one lives with.

Another name for this kind of paganism, a term we

hear more and more frequently today, is "civil religion." Civil religion is a religion whose morality is simply a reflection or an echo of what the "nice" people in one's culture think, say and do. Civil religion is respected in society: It supports all the values the society stands for. It is the religion of the tribe.

A man I know had a daughter who became pregnant. She was very, very young. He took her to their family doctor, a kind, ethical man. He was very understanding, very reasonable. He advised her "not to keep" the baby. He suggested a clinic where the pregnancy could be "terminated" very simply. It was a clean-suit kind of interview: air-conditioned office, well-dressed people, modulated voices and a very reasonable, civilized approach to the whole thing.

I spoke with the doctor later. I told him I understood and sympathized with his position. As a doctor he represented the technical culture of our civilization, our tribe. His social position held him up as one who had achieved what life in our country has to offer: He was educated, cultured, financially well-established, socially beyond reproach. It was natural that people would consult him about moral issues: He was a man you would expect to have right values, to be a custodian of the wisdom of our tribe. After all, he had "made it" in our society; he was one of the "right" kind of people. And in addition to this, his technical, medical knowledge made him the possessor of secrets. He knew things that others did not. People naturally presumed, in an unconscious way, that he also had a special knowledge of the secrets of God.

"You mean a witchdoctor," he said.

That's right. When he began to advise abortion he was assuming the role of the witchdoctor, presuming to pass judgments on life and death in the name of his position in society, in the name of the secret things he knew—which were not the secrets of God at all, but the technical data of the medical books. The fact he did not wear a bone in his nose or shake a rattle just threw people off guard—just as people are thrown off guard by the fact that our society has the technical knowledge to kill babies surgically and dispose of them discreetly in clinical garbage cans instead of letting them be born and exposing them to die on a mountainside.

The Sins of Our Day

Nice people in our society do not murder or steal—except in the ways that are acceptable to our society. Ralph Nader accuses Union Carbide of turning out air pollution from one plant in West Virginia that equals "one-third of all the particulate matter coming out of New York City in a year.

"People go around gasping for breath. Emphysema levels are up. Worker diseases are high. Union Carbide made $157 million in 1970 after taxes. A portion of those profits were obtained at the expense of the lungs and bodies of the men, women and children who live in and around those plants," he pointed out in *The New Yorker* (Oct. 8, 1973).

In 1965 Nader wrote the book *Unsafe at Any*

Speed, criticizing the automobile industry for unsafe designs in cars. In 1973 General Motors was obliged to recall 3,700,000 cars after Nader's repeated testimony that the steering mechanisms in Chevrolet, Pontiac, Buick and Oldsmobile models were defective. According to National Highway Traffic Safety Administration figures, the rise in traffic-accident deaths that had been on the increase until 1966, began to decline after the passage that year of the National Traffic and Motor Vehicle Safety Act (in which Nader's testimony played an important part).

It can hardly be disputed that Nader's attack on the industry's negligence helped save thousands of lives that otherwise would have been lost through—what shall we call it?—socially acceptable, industrial homicide. *The New Yorker* article on Nader's defense of consumers sounds like a commentary on the Ten Commandments as they should be applied to the modern world: Thou shalt not murder through industry, steal through unjust profits, lie through fraudulent advertising, or ignore the effect of your business practices upon your neighbor.

The point of all this is that people like the doctor and businessmen above would never think of themselves as being irreligious. It is the *nice* people who do these things—those who are known as and consider themselves to be "good Christians."

Who would treat the president of Eastern Airlines like a Philistine? And what has a nicer, more wholesome image in our society than the dairy industry? But both the president of Eastern Airlines and the president of the National Dairy Association have confessed that their associations paid thousands of dollars in illegal contributions to Richard Nixon's presidential campaign fund.

Do you think any of this ever comes up in confession? From my experience through 16 years of priesthood, I would say it does not. People just rarely think about confessing sins that do not go against the *civil* religion. These accepted business and social practices of our culture are referred to in the New Testament in condemnatory terms such as "the world."

It is those whom we call the "right kind of people" in our society who have managed to segregate themselves most effectively from other races and social classes. The "representative"—in this case the rich—members of society do not need to call names in the streets and throw bricks at minority groups like the rioting whites in South Boston. They can buy distance through real estate. As a rule they live in the suburbs and send their children to private schools. Those who are well-off never need to accuse themselves in confession of overt hostility toward minority groups. They are like people who have withdrawn into a castle, filled the moat with water, and pulled up the drawbridge. Within the castle they can honestly say, "I am nice to everyone," because they have managed to make sure that no group of people will ever get into the castle whom they might not feel inclined to be nice to.

The Leaven in the Dough

These are hard facts to face, hard questions to think about. And I'm not proposing any simple, much less simplistic, answers. But isn't it true that when we listen to a sermon, we are not really looking for the hard questions, for a challenge to our own moral *status quo*? Don't we rather listen for some reassuring affirmation of those things in society that keep our own position secure?

Things that threaten law and order (murder, overt theft and burglary, lying, disobedience to parents, marital infidelity and premarital sex)—these things we want religion to help stamp out. But we do not want religion, or its ministers, to step on our own toes, especially in business, politics and social life.

Yet a prophetic voice in our times, Vatican II, describes the role of the lay Christian as being that of an active leaven to lift up the dough of this world that tends downward by its own weight. It is precisely *in* the "ordinary circumstances of family and social life, of secular professions and occupations" that the lay Christian is to do his work for the Kingdom of God (*Constitution on the Church*, 31). The proper work of the laity is to penetrate the world of business, politics and social customs with the light of the gospel, to lift it up and transfigure it, to make Christ present in the secular sphere—in the real, everyday, workaday world—through the "testimony of a life resplendent in faith, hope, and charity" *(Decree on the Apostolate of the Laity*, 2).

The paradox is this: What many of us grew up expecting the Church to be for us is the exact opposite of what the Church now asks us to be for the world. The Church exhorts the laity, in the name of Christ, to go out and challenge the attitudes and values of society. But a vociferous portion of the laity gets angry if a priest challenges any of our attitudes or values at Mass.

The Church is not just a humanitarian or "social action" religion. The mystery of God and the mystical experience of our own redeemed life must be the core and the soul of Christian preaching and of Christians' understanding of themselves. That is why the whole subject and aim of this book is deep, vivifying *encounter with the person of Christ*. And we will dig searchingly into this subject in the following chapters.

But our experience of God is sterile unless it also becomes our expression to the world. As Mahalia Jackson once said, "Some people are so heavenly-minded they are no earthly good." A copyrighted National Catholic News Service story printed in the Diocese of Richmond's weekly newspaper brings out my point:

WASHINGTON (NC)—The young priest of the diocese of Lafayette, La., had come home to say a Sunday Mass in the parish of his youth, Blessed Sacrament on Chevy Chase Circle in Montgomery County, Maryland.

It came time for the homily, and the congregation sat before him, respectful, well-dressed, representative of the "second richest county in the United States."

The priest spoke on the Gospel narrative of the unjust steward, and recalled that the ordinary of the archdiocese, Patrick Cardinal O'Boyle of Washington, had sent a letter to the Montgomery County Council strongly urging it to adopt a fair housing ordinance.

The young priest told his listeners that federal agencies located in Montgomery County ran into difficulties because Negroes on their staffs could not find homes in the area. He made mention of liberals who were interested in correcting injustices when they were far away, but ignored them at home.

There was a cough. Then another. Then enough coughs to be truly noticeable.

A man stood up in the body of the church, and demanded to have the priest's attention. This silenced the coughing, and every other sound in the church.

"With all respect to the Blessed Sacrament," the man said in time, speaking into the quiet, "couldn't we do without a political talk, Father?"

There was quiet again, more than before.

Then someone clapped his hands. Another joined in. Then some more. The young priest stood silently at the podium.

Another man arose, and all eyes focused on him. "Speak on the moral issue, Father," he urged the young priest.

"Speak," others said. "Speak."

One or two persons left.

The quiet was heavy.

Then the young priest resumed. He spoke again of the unjust steward, and of fair housing. He seemed to give just about the sermon he had intended to give.

It wasn't long after that he was distributing Communion. Nearly everybody in the church approached the altar rail and received.

Where does this leave us? It leaves us wondering whether the image presented by the typical congregation at Mass is really the image of Christianity, or just the mummified face of an age-old "orthodox paganism." The teenager we spoke of in the beginning of this chapter put the problem very well: What makes it appear to so many that "the church is a mausoleum"?

Our churches do seem at times to be mausoleums—and the religion we find in them to be something of a mummy. If what we find expressed in church—or all that comes through to us, at least—is civil religion, an "orthodox paganism" of code and cult, then our religion as we experience it is not Christianity but a mummy. Mummies are easy to live with—they don't change their appearance or stir around very much; and they don't challenge people at all. But mummies are notoriously deficient in life. That is their weak point. And a religion that is deficient in life is a pretty dead issue.

The rest of this book is going to deal with the living Christ, the Christ who rose from the tomb, the Christ who "goes ahead of you" to Galilee (Mt 28: 7), who is way out in front, inviting his disciples to come follow him and give to others the good news of the Kingdom of God. It is going to deal with how one finds this Christ—not outside of the Church, but in the Church; inside and outside of the church building; in the midst of the People of God and of the world to which that People is sent.

But first I would like to ask you one question. And I would like you to answer it for yourself, but to answer it *in writing*. (After all, this is supposed to be a serious book!)

What if I Stopped Believing?

Take a pencil and paper and ask yourself, "If I stopped believing in Jesus Christ—and in the Bible—today, can I write down five concrete decisions I would make that would significantly affect my life tomorrow?"

It doesn't count to write down things like "I would lose all meaning in life" or "Nothing would make sense anymore." These are not decisions *you* make about things you will *do*; these are just effects you see happening *to* you.

And don't write down, "I would stop going to Mass on Sundays." You would naturally stop any act of cult that is precisely a way of saying you believe in Christ.

Just write down how your *life* would change; how *you would change it* by concrete choices tomorrow if you stopped believing in Jesus Christ today.

Remember, you still believe in God—in a Creator who made this world, who rewards the good and punishes the evil. You would hardly begin to chase every woman or man in town, or go out and start robbing filling stations just because you do not believe in Christ. The pagans who never heard of Christ have more sense than to do these things.

What would you change in your ordinary, everyday life just because you ceased to believe in Jesus Christ and in the Bible as God's Word?

What you write down will give you the measure of how conscious and real your Christianity is right now.

The Person of Christ in Your Life

CHAPTER TWO: *The Man at the Jordan*

John the Baptist had had a hard day. And it had been crowned with disappointment. All day long—and for weeks before that—he had been announcing the coming of the Messiah, the Savior, the "Lamb of God" who would take away the sins of the whole world. And the crowds were coming. They were flocking to be baptized as a sign of repentance.

But were they really getting the message? They had asked him what to do and he told them: Soldiers should stop bullying people. Tax collectors should stop cheating. Everyone should show a little love and generosity by sharing what he had with his neighbor. (See Lk 3.)

Yet that wasn't really what he was there for, to tell people *what to do*. He had come to tell them *whom to expect*. "There is one to come who is mightier than I. I am not fit to loosen his sandal strap. He will baptize you in the Holy Spirit and in fire" (Lk 3:16).

Then Jesus came. He came walking along the river-bank and John pointed him out. "Look," he said, "that's the one I've been talking about. That's the 'Lamb of God,' the one who takes away the sins of the world!"

And no one moved.

They just sat there. No one asked any questions, and no one got up to follow Jesus. They all just sat there, looking at him.

John couldn't understand it. Well, yes, he could when he thought about it. After all, in spite of all his preaching they still weren't prepared for what they saw. They had expected someone in the order of a hero—a conquering general, or a king on a white horse, or at least someone kind of dramatic like John himself with his camel's hair cutoffs and diet of nature foods. But what they saw was a per-fectly commonplace man from the country, just an ordinary citizen walking along on ground level.

They didn't know what to make of it.

It's not that they didn't believe John; they weren't denying that this was the Lamb of God. He was just so different from anything they had expected that they didn't know how to respond.

So they did what most people do when they don't know how to respond: They just sat there.

John's Gospel tells us: "The next day John was there again with two of his disciples. As he watched Jesus walk by [a second time] he said, 'Look! There is the Lamb of God!' The two disciples heard what he said, and followed Jesus" (1:35-37).

We can reconstruct the scene: The two disciples—their names were John (who wrote the Gospel) and Andrew—were just as uncertain of how to act as they had been the day before. But this time they felt they had to do *something*. John looked at Andrew and said, "What are we going to do?" Andrew shrugged his shoulders and answered, "I don't know. Let's go see." So they got up and began walking along the riverbank behind Jesus.

We can stop right here for a moment and point out that what John and Andrew did is typical of every authentic faith response. Jesus usually comes into our lives in a form we were not expecting. Our first reaction, therefore, is not to respond at all. We read a word in the Gospels, we hear a suggestion in a sermon, which we just weren't prepared to receive. It stuns us a little, leaves us flabbergasted. Our first inclination is to dismiss it. Usually we do, and sometimes that is the end of it.

But sometimes Jesus comes again. With some people he seems to insist, to keep walking by until they feel they have to do *something* about what they are experiencing—one way or the other.

Still they don't know what to do. But if they are willing to take a *first step*, not insisting on knowing where it will lead, Jesus will take it from there.

He did this with John and Andrew. When he noticed them walking along behind him, he turned around and asked them a question.

It seems to be a very simple question. But in reality it is the most profound question anyone can ask a man about himself. It is the question God asks every man who comes into this world—sooner or later. And until he asks it, and we answer it, we are not mature as human beings or as believers in God.

"When Jesus turned around and noticed them following him, he asked them: *'What are you looking for?'*" (Jn 1:38, italics added).

Jesus' Question: "What Are You Looking for?"

What are you looking for in life? What do you want out of existence? What do you want your life to mean?

Until we have answered that question (of course, it is not definitively and completely answered until we breathe our final word at death), we have not yet created ourselves *as persons*.

God creates us as human beings, as human natures. But from the moment we begin to exist, we begin to create ourselves—with his help—as persons.

Our *human nature* is what we speak of in answer to the question, "*What* are you?" We are human beings, men, women. But our *person* is what we talk about in answer to the question, "*Who* are you?" We begin by giving our name.

But what is our name? In itself it is a nonsense syllable. It doesn't really have any meaning except what we give it by our lives. What a man's name means—what it will finally mean when it is written on his tombstone—is the sum total, the cumulative result, of *all the free responses this man has made to life*: to things, to himself, to other persons, to God.

Each time a human being chooses to respond to life in a deliberate way, he breathes a "word" of self-creation. God in the beginning said, "Let it be," and the world was; likewise man, every time he breathes a word of deliberate choice, says, "Let it be," and by that very fact his person is.

And so, when God asks man, "What are you looking for?," he is in reality asking man his name. He is asking, "Who are you? Whom do you choose to be? How do you want to direct your life? What, or whom, do you choose as your destiny?"

Our temptation at this point is to give the answer we learned in the catechism: "Lord, I want to know you, to love you and to serve you in this life and to be happy with you forever in the next!"

This is a good answer, but not to the question Jesus asks. Jesus did not ask, "What *should* you be looking for?" or "What does the catechism *say* you should be looking for?" He asks, "What *are* you looking for?"

And this question cannot be answered with words.

At this point we are tempted to start speculating. We try casting around in our minds for an answer, asking ourselves what we really *think*, what we really *believe* is the meaning, the purpose of life. We want to answer by analyzing our motives and telling the Lord what we think our real attitudes and values are.

Useless! The only real way to answer the question we are asked is to point. Point at our lives. Point to those things, those choices in our lives, those realities in our life-style that *tell* what we are really looking for in life.

When it comes to answering the most fundamental question of life, every person must be mute. We cannot answer for ourselves; we can only call witnesses to answer for us. And our only witnesses are our choices—our choices as they have found expression in the world around us.

A choice that remains completely inside a man's head or heart has not found its full reality as a choice. For a choice to be truly creative of us as persons, it must be a *word-made-flesh* in action.

God himself accepted these terms when he chose to reveal himself to man. When asked his name God replied, "I am who am." But this could never be adequately expressed in mere words. So God waited until his Word was made flesh. Then he spoke again: "God is love," he said and *pointed* to the body of his Son upon the cross.

So, to answer the question, "What are you looking for?," we must point to our life. How do we spend our time? How do we spend our money? How do we express ourselves through our dress? Through what we eat and drink? Our work? What does our house or room say about us? What does our selection of friends say about our real objectives in life? Why did we marry this particular person? Does the life we live together really express an overriding desire to spend our time on this earth getting to know and love God better, and serving him with all our strength in everything we do?

A concrete way to ask whether we really live to know, love and serve the Lord is to ask ourselves why we got up this morning. What determined the time of our rising? Did we check our starting time at work and count backwards through driving time, breakfast, dressing time, and set the alarm there? If so, then let us say quite simply and frankly that we got up this morning to go to work, and let it go at that. But if we counted backwards from work through driving, breakfast and dressing to a period given first thing in the morning to praising the Lord, reading his word in Scripture, and seeking to know him through prayer, then we can say we got up this morning to know, love and serve the Lord.

Encounter with Christ begins when the Lord asks us, in some form or another (as he may be asking you anew through this book), "What are you looking for?"

The disciples, John and Andrew, were caught off guard. When Jesus turned around and asked his question, they didn't know what to say. John nudged Andrew; Andrew nudged John. Finally one of them stammered out the first thing that came into his mind: "Rabbi (which means Teacher), where do you stay?" (Jn 1:38).

Our Question: "Where Do You Dwell?"

"Where do you dwell?" For all our intellectual casting about, for all our planning and running around, we have only to listen to our heart. There we will hear the answer—not to what *we* are, in fact, looking for (only our life can tell us that), but to what our *heart* is looking for, what our very being cries out for: We want to experience God.

This is what religion is all about. Not morality (although it must include this). Not a system of laws and observances. Not a yearly schedule of "courtesy calls" to God. But *communion*. Encounter with the living God. "Lord, where do you dwell?" Real, experienced, intimate knowledge of God as Person.

Christianity is knowledge of God as he is in himself, and not just as he can be known through analysis of the things he has created. By studying the created universe, including the human creature, we can figure out a lot about God the Creator, God the Great Designer, God the Bountiful Giver. We can find indications of his power, his goodness, his wisdom. We can learn something about *what* God is.

But we get no hint of *who* he is. We cannot know his name.

By analyzing the way creatures are put together and the parts they are provided with, we can figure out the plan and the principles God followed in producing them. We can discern their purpose and the way of acting that is natural and proper to them.

But we can know nothing of the way of acting that is proper to God.

A chair is obviously designed to be sat upon. We can know that the person who produced it intended people to sit down. But of that person himself we cannot know whether he sits, stands or floats in the air. A chair tells us what its designer intended the chair to do; it does not tell us what the designer does himself.

And likewise there are natural philosophies and pagan religions that can tell us a lot about how God intended *us* to live, and how he wants *us* to act. But they cannot tell us about the life of God himself or about God's own personal way of acting.

To be holy as God is holy; to love not as man should but as God does—this is reserved for those who have come to know the Father through the revelation of Jesus Christ.

And this is really what Christianity is all about. "Eternal life is this: to know you, the only true God, and him whom you have sent, Jesus Christ" (Jn 17:3).

We begin to be Christians, consciously, the moment we start asking Jesus, "Teacher, where do you dwell?" It is when we begin to desire, and to choose, and to act upon the choice to *know the Lord* that we begin to be followers of Christ.

To know the Lord does not mean to know *about* him. It means to *know* him, to encounter his living, acting mind and will and to respond with understanding and appreciation. It means to "acquire a fresh, spiritual way of thinking. You must put on that new man" (Eph 4:23-24).

The Christian is a person who has taken on, and is striving to take on, the way of thinking, judging and appreciating things proper to Jesus Christ. The Christian has "put on" the mind of Christ; the Christian is a person who thinks like God.

This is obviously "news" in any age. People who go around thinking like God are apt to be upsetting— as Jesus himself was upsetting. For some God's way of thinking is bad news; for others it is good news—*the* Good News, in fact. But for everybody it should be news.

And if it isn't news, it isn't the mind of God.

John the Baptist at the Jordan was not preaching a religion of rules—as if Jesus came only to give a new and enlarged version of the Ten Commandments. He was not preaching a religion of *contract*— a fixed agreement between God and man where each is bound to do certain clearly specified things and where each can deal with the terms of the contract rather than with the other as a person. John was preaching a religion of *covenant*, whereby two persons agree to *keep acting toward each other as persons* according to the nature of their relationship.

In this case the nature of the relationship is spousal: God has revealed himself to his Church as to his Bride. He has opened to her—and to each member who desires to receive him—all the secrets of his heart. He has held nothing back. He wants to share everything he thinks and feels, all his deepest appreciations and aspirations with us. He wants to draw us into intimate communion and understanding with himself, into the deepest participation in his own most interior life.

This is the covenant he offers us. It is like marriage, where two people do not know ahead of time what they will be asked to give and do for one another. They bind themselves simply to love each other with their whole hearts, to try to get to know each other through deep—if sometimes painful—communication all of their lives, to give up all of their selfishness for one another. It would be impossible for marriage partners to spell out in advance in concrete, cut-and-dried terms all that each will expect to do for and receive from the other. Spouses do not present to each other a list of mummified *what's* to observe; they present a living *who* to interact with.

And this is what Jesus offers. This is what John stood by the Jordan to proclaim: not *what* men were to do, but *whom* they were to expect.

When the disciples John and Andrew asked Jesus, "Where do you live?," meaning "Where does God dwell?," his answer came back as no answer, and yet as the only answer possible.

Had Jesus been a Dominican he would have replied, perhaps, as a learned follower of St. Thomas Aquinas: "God does not dwell in a place; he is infinite spirit, present everywhere, and yet confined nowhere at the same time." And he would have gone on with a lesson in philosophy.

Had Jesus been a Franciscan, he would most probably have answered: "God dwells among the simple things, among the birds and the flowers of nature, among the poor of the world. Go out into the fields, go out to the poor, and you will find him."

Had Jesus been a Jesuit, we know what his answer would have been: "Come to one of our schools, and we will teach you all about him."

But Jesus, fortunately, was not a Dominican, not a Franciscan, not a Jesuit. He was only Jesus. And his answer was: *"Come and see."*

In the following chapters of this book we will take up the Lord's invitation, "Come and see." We will ask how one goes about doing this. What follows, then, will not teach you about Christ. It will not even teach you how to learn about him. It will tell you *how to meet him.*

Reaching an Adult Level of Prayer

CHAPTER THREE: *How to Talk to Your Aunt Matilda*

The first step in meeting anyone is to *talk* to him. We can enter into relationship with other persons to the degree we are able to *communicate* deeply with other persons, to talk sincerely about ourselves, our feelings, our innermost desires and values.

But for real relationship to exist, the communication must be mutual. We must also be able to *listen*: to be interested in the other person, to understand what he or she is saying and to empathize with it, to respond with our hearts as well as with our minds, to take a stance toward the other person and make commitments.

The Stages of Communicating—and Praying

Little babies do not know how to talk. One measure of a person's growth is the measure of his ability to express himself.

When we were little children our parents taught us how to talk. When Aunt Matilda came to the door, mother would tell us, "Say 'Hello, Aunt Matilda,' " and we would parrot back, with exactly the same inflection she used, "Hello, Aunt Matilda."

And so we learned phrases: "Hello, Aunt Matilda." "Thank you, Aunt Matilda." "Goodbye, Aunt Matilda." Not bad for a beginner.

But if, at the age of 16, all a boy or girl could say was "Hello, Aunt Matilda," "Thank you, Aunt Matilda," Aunt Matilda would wonder if something were wrong with the child.

Memorized phrases are the way people learn to speak. They are necessary. They are meant to teach us the attitudes, the values we should adopt and express toward another person. As these attitudes and values become our own and as others are added to them, however, we should begin to be able to express them in our own words. This is a sign we are catching on, assimilating what we have learned, becoming adult.

With prayer it is the same. Prayer is communicating with God. When we were little we learned prayers— that is, we memorized formulas. We learned to say, "God bless Mommy and Daddy, Joey and Martha, Grandpa and Grandma, Aunt Matilda . . ." Perhaps we also added the cat, the dog and the teddy bear. This was fine. When we started tossing in a few blessables of our own it was a sign we were catching on to the system.

Then we graduated to adult formulas—that is, grown-up prayers. We didn't always understand what we were saying, but little by little the concepts sank in. I still remember the day when I mastered enough grammar to stop wondering who "thy womb Jesus" was. Later I learned that other children had had difficulties just like mine: "Our Father who art in heaven, Harold is thy name. . ." "Give us this day our jelly bread. . ." "And lead us not into Penn Station. . ." "Pray for us, poor Spanish children of Eve. . ."

Now I am a priest, a religious—a real professional—and I am only just beginning to understand the meaning of some of the psalms I have been reciting for 15 years.

The trouble is, many of us are stuck on the level of memorized prayers. We need not ever stop saying the prayers we learned: There will always be more in them than we are able to really make our own. But we must not limit our prayer to "prayers." Memorized phrases should not be the only medium through which we communicate with God. We shouldn't subject God to "Hello, Aunt Matilda" all our lives.

The next stage of growth, then, after memorized prayers is to talk to God in *your own words*. Just go into the church or sit down on your bed and talk to him. Talk to him as Father, as Teacher, as Savior, as indwelling Guide, as Healer, Comforter, Friend. Just be yourself with him: You can both be more comfortable that way.

Even though I will pass on rather quickly to the next stage of prayer, I do not want to give the impression this one is unimportant. It should continue all our lives. In fact, no matter what form of prayer we are using, we should generally spend some time—interspersed throughout our prayer, or at the end of it—talking to God in our own words. In the spiritual books this is called a "colloquy." And when it is done out loud with others, it is called "shared prayer." We should do more of it.

We will speak more about shared prayer toward the end of this book. But right now I want to talk about the third stage that our prayer—or our communication with anybody—should reach. This is the stage of *listening*.

A compulsive talker cannot enter into relationships. The compulsive talker is not interested in communicating with anybody or forming relationships; only in releasing tension. The compulsive talker talks to "get something off his chest," so that he will feel better.

We do this with God. And it is not always wrong. A person is not really called a compulsive talker unless that is the only way he *can* talk. But to go in to a friend, or to God, on some occasions just to let off steam, to blow up, to break down, or to think out loud—this is perfectly normal. It is one of the things friendship is all about.

But it is just one of the things. Real friendship, real relationship with another, is a two-way street. We talk *and* we listen. We express ourselves to one who is interested in who we are; and we listen to another express himself or herself, because we are interested in who this person is. We want to know *each other*— which is different from just knowing or being known.

What is the kind of prayer that lets us really both *know* God and *be known* by him in deep, personal relationship? This kind of prayer could be called by many names and has been called by many names in the history of spirituality. Let us just begin by calling it the *prayer of encounter*.

Encountering Others—and God

We encounter God the way we encounter human beings.

The first step in an encounter is to really *confront* what another is saying or doing. This is not quite the same as just paying attention. I can listen attentively to something you say to me, hear and understand every word of it, but just not choose to confront its significance at all. To "confront," as we use the word here, means to *really listen* as opposed to just letting someone's words come in without registering. But it also means more than that. It means a positive choice to follow up on what we have heard, to pursue the topic further until we can make some personal response of our own to what the other has said.

To "confront" another in this sense does not mean to *challenge* him. Sometimes we think of confrontation in terms of eyeball-to-eyeball, chin-jutting disagreement. It means rather to *let oneself be challenged* by what another has said: to accept the challenge of *understanding* it, the challenge of *responding* to it, the challenge of taking a *stance* toward it.

Suppose I meet you for the first time at a cocktail party. You say to me, "How are you?" I answer, "Fine." (So far we haven't said anything; we're just tossing words back and forth to warm up.) Then you say, "Did you have a nice trip up from Alabama?" I answer, "No, I was in a wreck on the freeway."

Now, at this point, you have an option. You can confront what I said or you can choose not to. You have understood the words; you were paying attention. But it may be you weren't *really asking* me whether I had a nice trip up from Alabama. Maybe your question was just another warm-up pitch. I, however, chose to confront your question; I took it as a real pitch and put a bat into it. Now it is coming back to you, and we will find out whether you really want to play ball.

Suppose you say, "Oh, that is too bad. Well, it's good you're here now, anyway."

You have just decided not to go for the ball I batted you. You choose not to confront the fact that I am a man standing before you who has just had a wreck on the freeway. You are not interested in my wreck on the freeway. This probably means you are not interested in me.

If you were interested in me, interested in getting to know me, you would *take up* the topic of my wreck on the freeway. You would want to know what that wreck meant to *me*, how I experienced it, how I responded to it. And through this you would be getting to know more about what kind of *person* I am: You would understand "where I'm coming from," "where I'm at."

Suppose you do choose to confront me—the me standing before you in the freshness of my own lived experience. What would you do?

You would go to the next step: You would *ask questions*. These would not be just any kind of questions, but questions addressed to the reality of my freeway wreck, explicitly designed to let you *make connections* between my experience and your own experience.

You might ask, for example, "How did it happen?" You are not really asking the cause of the accident as such, the way a highway patrolman or an automobile safety-design enthusiast might. (If that is your interest, the rest of the conversation will be about the technicalities of safe driving and automobile design, and we will never get to know one another.) You are asking about the details of the accident in order to get a clearer picture of the concrete reality *I have experienced*. You are trying to get to something in my experience, or in my response, that *you can relate to*. Then you will be able to relate to me in the reality of my own lived, personal life.

At this stage of our encounter, you keep asking questions until something I say calls for a value-response from you. It may be an idea that you have to decide whether you agree with. Or it may be an attitude or value that you admire or disapprove of.

In all of this you will be getting to know me as a person who *sees* things a certain way and *responds* to them in a certain way. And since you also, as a person, are a seer and a responder, you will have to call yourself into question and take a deeper look at your own stance toward the reality of this world. My attitude toward the world may confirm you in your own stance, or cause you to modify it. In any case, our encounter has been real if, through it, you have deepened, confirmed, modified, reversed, or in any way been affected in the reality of your own free response to this world—to things, to people and to God. You "know" me, because you know yourself to be personally affected by me.

If my reality has not affected you in any way, then you do not really know me as a person. We cannot confront the value of another's free response to life without confronting at the same time the value of our own.

And this brings us to the third stage required for real encounter: You have to *take a stance* with your will toward the other person's reality. You cannot do this, of course, except through taking a stance toward what that person has said or done.

Your stance does not have to be agreement or dis-agreement on every particular issue. You may not know yet whether you agree or disagree. In dealing with another human being you may make a definite choice to refrain from judging something said or done. (I'm not sure one can take a stance like this with regard to God, however.) The important point is not the kind of stance one takes, but that one must *take* a stance, and take it *consciously*, if a relationship with another is going to be real.

Suppose that in the course of your questions about my wreck on the freeway I tell you I was pinned under my car for an hour while dozens of cars went by, their drivers looking at me out of the window, and every one of them refusing to stop. Suppose you ask how I feel about this and I reply, "I feel very, very bitter. If I ever see another person in an accident, you can be sure I won't stop; not if I am the last person left on the earth!"

What would you do then?

If you say something noncommittal like, "Well, that is a very interesting attitude," and change the subject, what would it mean? You choose not to pursue our relationship further. You don't want to get involved. You don't want to get involved with the issue, because you don't want to get involved with me—at least, not now. I have expressed my stance toward reality—part of it, anyway. But you choose not to take, or express, a stance toward that reality or toward me. You back off by changing the subject.

If, on the other hand, you do choose in turn to express your stance toward what I have said, then we are in relationship. We may be in agreement or in disagreement, but *we are interacting with one another*. We are letting our realities confront and be confronted by one another in a full sense—not just *initially*, as when we first began to talk; not just *halfway*, as when we asked and answered questions and made connections between our experience; but *all the way to term*, by expressing freely the stance we choose to take as self-determining persons toward the reality of one another.

If we take a stance toward one another, the relationship is real, and it can go on from there. We can argue, fight, agree, celebrate, accept, tolerate, love or despise one another. But we do not ignore each other's reality. We are in *contact* with one another as persons. We are *news* to one another.

These are the three stages, then, of the kind of dialogue between persons that leads to real encounter, real relationship. We must *confront* what the other is saying; *ask questions* that will enable us to relate what is said to our own experience; and *take a stance* toward what we see.

The Prayer of Encounter

The *prayer of encounter* with God consists of these same three stages. Ever since God became man in

Jesus Christ, it has been possible to deal with him as a human being, to come to know him in a human way, to communicate with him the way we communicate with other human beings. In Jesus we have God in human form, speaking human words, performing human acts, expressing himself through human gestures. We can respond to the Person of God by responding to his human expression of himself, and so enter into personal relationship with him.

The starting point for this prayer is Scripture, especially the Gospels, the Acts of the Apostles and the Epistles of the New Testament. For most of us, I think, the Gospels are the place to begin.

In reading Scripture we should keep in mind two things:

1) *This is the Word of God.*

Several different literary forms are used in the Scriptures, from straight historical narrative to parables or stories made up to illustrate a point. There are figures of speech, rhetorical exaggerations, even humor. But *God is the author* of everything in the Scriptures. Nothing there is more or less his word; all is his word.

Consequently, in reading Scripture, we should be aware, with great reverence, that we are listening to the voice of God. He is expressing his mind through a variety of human literary forms, speaking to us with all the different approaches and nuances of meaning that people use in communicating with one another. But God is the one who is speaking.

2) *God speaks through the Scriptures now.*

God is not dead. The Scriptures are not just a book—all we have left to help us know him. No, God is very much alive and communicating with us today. The same Holy Spirit who worked in the hearts of those who wrote the Scriptures works in our hearts as we read them, inspiring us to understand their meaning—at least the meaning God wants to convey to each of us today.

God does not inspire every person reading the Scriptures with some personal gift of infallibility. But he *communicates* through the Scriptures with every person who reads them, provided that person is open and able to hear.

This is a distinction very frequently misunderstood, and confusion about it keeps many persons—especially Catholics—from ever reading the Scriptures. We Catholics have been warned so much against "private interpretation" of the Scriptures that we fear to interpret them at all. Our tendency is—or was—to leave the Scriptures to the theologians and to live our lives by the catechism.

There is a very healthy humility in this, but there is also a very tragic misunderstanding of what reading the Scriptures is all about. The Scriptures can be read in two ways:

1) *To proclaim the Word of God.*

The first way, or purpose, of reading the Scriptures is to proclaim the Word of God—to teach, to pass on the Good News of Christ. It is in this context we are warned against the danger of "private interpretation."

No private individual is authorized or qualified, as an individual, to proclaim to the world the authentic meaning of God's Word as it is found in the Scriptures. It is the Church, and the Church alone, who can authentically interpret, explain and teach the meaning and message of the Scriptures. And the Church does this, not through private individuals—even prophets—but through persons with public office in the Church: the pope and the bishops, primarily, with the assistance of the priests and theologians, religious and lay catechists, CCD instructors and so on, who are in union with them and respect their interpretative norms. (The prophets blow bugles, but in the last analysis, it is the hierarchy who directs the orchestra.)

When Catholics were warned in the "old days" against the dangers of reading the Bible, it was in the historical context of the Protestant Reformation and its aftermath. Because of the foolish debates and bitter arguments going on between Protestants and Catholics, people were running to the Scriptures, not as to a well from which to drink, but as to a rock quarry from which to pick out stones to throw at their adversaries. People were not receiving scriptural texts reverently, like bread. They were hurling them at each other furiously, like projectiles. In this atmosphere the Church warned Catholics against the presumption of reading the Scriptures with a view toward coming up with one's own personal and definitive statement about the real meaning of the Christian revelation.

2) *For personal nourishment and inspiration.*

Another way of reading the Scriptures—the normal way, and the way we are proposing here—is to read them for one's own personal nourishment and inspiration. One doesn't presume to know the objective meaning of everything that is said. Nor is one looking for the objective meaning in every instance. One is simply reading the Scriptures as a way of listening to God, confident that *something* in what one reads will speak to one's heart, will be the word one needs to hear for one's own life right now.

In many instances the thought or inspiration one receives from a passage of Scripture will not be the objective meaning or purpose of the passage at all, and one will be quite aware of this. A man reads, for example, "Let us go up to the house of the Lord" just when he has been fighting for days the growing conviction that it is time to go to confession. And the text hits him like a ton of bricks. So he goes to confession, and finds great grace and profit in it.

Does this mean that this scriptural text, when written, had anything to do with confession? No. But it does mean that *God spoke through it* to *this person* at *this time* to move him to confession. This was what *he* needed to hear, and God used his own human words in Scripture to get through to him.

The Church has always been extremely conscious of God speaking through the Scriptures with a living voice today. This is why the Church has always venerated the Scriptures with a reverence like that shown to the real presence of Christ in the Eucharist.

As the *Constitution on Divine Revelation* says: "The Church has always venerated the divine Scriptures just as she venerates the body of the Lord, since from the table of both the word of God and of the body of Christ she unceasingly receives and offers to the faithful the bread of life, especially in the sacred liturgy" (21).

Therefore, the Council specifically urges all Christians "to learn by frequent reading of the divine Scriptures the 'excelling knowledge of Jesus Christ' (Phil 3:8). For ignorance of the Scriptures is ignorance of Christ" (*Constitution on Divine Revelation*, 25).

If we want to enter into relationship with Christ, then, to encounter him ever more deeply as a person, the way to do this is by reflecting and praying over the Scriptures.

Next question: How does one pray over the Scriptures?

A Practical Method for Praying Over the Scriptures

CHAPTER FOUR: *I'd Walk a Mile For a Roman*

We are going to present here a very easy method of praying over the Scriptures. It is easy, at least, in the sense that it is fool-proof: You can't fail to pray authentically if you follow the method. But we don't promise that prayer itself will be easy. It may be, and it may not be. That is between you and God. All we can guarantee is that it will be rewarding if you persevere in it and respond to the challenges you find.

The kind of prayer we are presenting here is the *prayer of encounter*. It is a way of getting to know God as a person, and of getting to know him better.

Let us begin with a definition. The prayer of encounter is *reflecting on the Word of God until we come to decisions that change our lives.*

The change in our life may be great or small, from buying a different kind of shoelace to selling all we own and moving out to the desert. But there must be a change. Prayer that does not affect our life is simply not prayer, no matter how "good it feels."

Now let's see how we do it.

The Flight Plan

We prepare for this kind of prayer by reading something in Scripture. I would suggest you start with one of the Gospels. Some people take one of the four Gospels and pray their way right through it. Others borrow a missalette out of their parish church and pray each day over the Gospel reading for Mass. (The Gospel text itself won't be in the missalette, but if you look under the Mass of the day, it will tell you were to find it: which Gospel, which chapter, which verses.)

If you don't find a system that works for you, consult the nearest priest or nun who looks holy. Priests and sisters are supposed to know how to pray. If you happen to hit on one who doesn't, he or she will probably be too embarrassed to admit it, and will look up the information necessary to help you.

How much should one read as preparation for one day's prayer? Not much—usually just the recounting of a single incident or event in Our Lord's life:

one miracle story, one parable, one idea that he preached.

And while you read it, *underline*. (For this reason I recommend you buy a paperback edition of the Bible. Put the expensive, hardcover one with pictures on a table and write the birthdays of your children in the front. But for your "working Bible," buy a cheap one).

The reason for underlining is that it helps you psychologically to pick out words or statements you want—or ought—to confront. If you are looking for something to underline, you will be alert to what is significant, to what strikes you as pretty good at first glance, or as pretty bad. This is the kind of thing to pray over.

Sometimes a word or phrase will kind of "jump out" at you; it will "hit" you. Underline that and pray over it. Sometimes a phrase or sentence will just confuse you; you won't know what it means. Mark that in another way and look for an explanation when you have a chance. Some people invest in a biblical commentary just for this purpose, but wait on that until you have a little experience. You can always call your pastor—or that nun again—and ask one of them what it means. (If you are interested in a reference book of your own, a standard one is the *Jerome Biblical Commentary*, published by Prentice-Hall.)

Some people read Scripture just before they pray over it. Others read the Scripture passage the night before, reread it again in the morning, and pray over it later in the day. Either way is good. If you do pray early in the morning, however, it is wise to read the Scripture the night before so it will have time to settle—and perhaps to work on you a little— as you sleep.

Before you can actually start to pray, you have to decide *where* you are going to be. This might sound silly, but it is a fact of human nature that people cannot do anything unless they are someplace. And the place where you are when you pray has a lot to do with how well you are going to pray. So choose it ahead of time. Don't wait until it is time to pray and then start looking for a quiet corner.

For people who don't happen to live in a monastery—and this includes the great majority of the world's population—finding a place to pray might not be so easy. Between the TV in the living room, the kids' voices all over the house and the wife's stockings hanging up in the bathroom, a "prayer corner" may not be easy to come by.

Good. That gives you a chance to exercise some ingenuity.

Time is also a problem. I have known women who prayed after lunch, when the morning's work is over and the kids are not yet home from school. Some men stop off in a church on the way home from work. Early morning is an option, and so is late at night. Another possibility many people don't think of is the middle of the night: Get up, pray and go back to bed again. You will have to find the time that is possible and practical for you. I would suggest, however, that you try to make your prayer at the same time each day if possible. There is something settling about rhythm in our lives.

All right. You have a time and place picked out for prayer. You have read a passage of Scripture and underlined what seems significant to you. You have listened to something Jesus said, or looked at something he did which really expressed his heart, and picked out something you want to confront. (Sometimes what you confront will be the whole passage, the whole account of something Jesus said or did, searching for its significance in your own life). Now you are ready to pray.

Taxiing Out to the Runway

We should never actually begin our prayer (or our Scripture reading) without taking a few moments just to get ourselves into the right frame of mind. Perhaps this is the time it takes to get our blood pressure down to normal.

Olympic contestants "psyche themselves up" for an event. Some people prepare for prayer by "turning off the switches." The essential thing is to get oneself ready to think, not on the plane of the ordinary, distracting business of the day, but on the plane of the transcendent reality of God.

A friend of mine who is a Zen teacher told me that you cannot get into a Buddhist temple without passing through a garden. The garden serves to quiet your mind from the hustle and bustle of the street. As you walk through the garden you prepare to enter into another world, another dimension of reality.

And so, when we are on our way to pray, we should begin anticipating a little—the way we do on our way to a party. We think about the fact that we are going to encounter God. We try to get up an appetite for the things he may have in store for us.

Revving Up the Engine

When we arrive at the place we have chosen for prayer, the first thing to do is *recall the presence of God*. Just remember he is with you, around you, within you.

God is present always—everywhere. But from our perspective he is not present *to us* unless we recall that he is there. So the first thing we do is "put" ourselves into his presence by a conscious act of awareness that we are standing before his face.

Next, we must *make some physical act of recognition* that God is there. Put your hand on your heart for a moment, or bow your head, or close your eyes. When I was a novice we were taught to kneel down and kiss the floor, more or less in the spirit of God's instruction to Moses when he spoke from the burning bush: "Come no nearer! Remove the sandals from your feet, for the place where you stand is holy ground" (Ex 3:5).

The point is that we have to *deal with God in a human way*. It is not human to come into someone's presence and give no external sign that we

recognize who and what he is, no visible indication
of the relationship we acknowledge and accept
between ourselves and him. If you are reading and
your wife comes into the room, you give her a
smile, maybe even a hug. If your boss walks in, you
take your feet off the desk. If a woman comes into
a room, men stand up.

With God we have to be just as human. To consciously "give" him recognition where we are by
entering into deliberate awareness of his presence,
we have to acknowledge his presence with our
bodies as well as with our minds. We work as whole
people.

While you are acknowledging God's presence with
your body, say a prayer in your heart: *Ask his help
to understand and respond to his Word.* Ask this in
your own words. But if you want to see how the
pros prayed for help to understand the things of
God, just to get an idea of the style of the thing,
read Solomon's prayer for wisdom, which is chapter nine of the Book of Wisdom. It begins:

> God of my fathers, Lord of mercy,
>> you who have made all things by your
>>> word . . . .
> Give me Wisdom, the attendant at your throne,
>> and reject me not from among your children;
> For I am your servant. . .a man weak and short-
>> lived
>> and lacking in comprehension of judgment
>>> and of laws.

To begin with a prayer like this reminds us we are
not setting out to master the Scriptures as a scholar

would. Nor do we come into God's presence to
talk things over with him as equals, in the sense
that we will decide for ourselves what to accept
and what not to accept out of the things he has to
say. With God we don't swap points of view. We
sit at his feet in humility and we listen, trying to
comprehend.

Nicodemus made this mistake: He came to Jesus
by night, thinking he was doing him a favor. Nicodemus was an important man, a public figure. Jesus
was just a young rabbi, and a controversial one at
that. Nicodemus didn't think he could afford to be
seen talking to Jesus, but he did want to give the
young man a hearing, and perhaps a little encouragement. He also thought he might learn from him—
and perhaps clarify Our Lord's thinking, too, out of
his own wisdom and experience. He was looking
forward to a stimulating theological discussion,
and he began—a bit condescendingly, perhaps—by
paying Jesus a compliment: "Rabbi, . . .we know
you are a teacher come from God, for no man can
perform signs and wonders such as you perform
unless God is with him" (Jn 3:2).

And Jesus cut him off at the knees with a reply
that looks like the baldest *non sequitur* in the Gospels: "I solemnly assure you, no one can see the
reign of God unless he is begotten from above"
(3:3).

Nicodemus was nonplussed. He became even more
confused as Jesus continued: "No one can enter
into God's kingdom without being begotten of

water and Spirit. . . . The wind blows where it will. You hear the sound it makes, but you do not know where it comes from or where it goes. So it is with everyone who is begotten of the Spirit" (3:5, 8).

By this time poor old Nicodemus couldn't do anything but stammer. So Our Lord just laughed and said to him, "You hold the office of teacher of Israel, and still you do not understand these matters?" (3:10).

Then they got down to business. Jesus explained to him, gently but unequivocally, that he wasn't there to discuss. He was there to bear witness to what he—and he alone—knew: "I solemnly assure you, we are talking about what we know, we are testifying to what we have seen. . . ." (3:11).

To enter into dialogue with Christ is to approach him as a disciple. The disciple knows that what the Teacher is saying is true. He may not understand it. He may ask questions about it. He can even raise difficulties against it. He just can't forget for a moment that he is a learner speaking with one who is in possession of the Truth.

When we enter into dialogue with God, the essential requirements are *humility* and *faith*. To the man who knows he "hasn't got it made"—who is "poor in spirit"—will be given the Kingdom of God.

What we have just been describing is the *vestibule of prayer*. Now we are ready to enter into the temple and talk to the Lord. We have had our appetizer, the salad dish. Now we come to the main course. It is time to get down to business. We are in place on the runway, our engines are revving, it is time to take off.

The Take-Off

The prayer of encounter consists essentially in going through the three phases of dialogue described in the last chapter. We *confront* something the Lord has said; we *make connections* by asking questions about it until we can relate it to our own experience; and we *take a stance* toward what we have seen, toward him.

1) *Confronting*

Confronting the Word of the Lord is not a very common thing in our culture—perhaps in any culture. God's Word is too familiar to us: It has gone in and out of our heads so many times that we don't feel its rough edges any more. Like a tire that has lost its tread, it rolls across our minds without leaving a trace. It doesn't bite into us.

So we have to make it bite. We have to remind ourselves that this is the Word of God, and that he is talking to us—to *me*.

One way to do this is to read a passage from Scripture and ask, "What effect has this had on my life?"

Take, for example, the text we are so familiar with: "If anyone wants to go to law over your shirt, hand him your coat as well. Should anyone press you into service for one mile, go with him two miles" (Mt 5:40-41). "When someone slaps you on one cheek, turn and give him the other" (Lk 6:29).

I had read this text for years without ever confronting it. One day I did confront it, and realized immediately that no one had ever taken me to court to sue me for my shirt. And if someone had, I am sure I would not have told him to take my coat for good measure!

Imagine that someone runs into your car, legally parked, and wants to sue you for the damage to *his* fender. Would you volunteer to pay for his fender and throw in the price of a new paint job as well? Or if someone holds you up on the street and takes away your money, would you call him back and say, "Hey, buddy, you forgot my watch!"

And who has ever forced you to walk a mile with him?

Roman law allowed occupying troops to demand this of local citizens in the Roman Empire as a convenient means of getting around in a strange locale. They had no service stations in those days handing out road maps, and a Roman in Palestine who was a little slow on Hebrew had a hard time finding his way. So the Roman soldiers used to pick up any citizen they met—out of his field, out of his shop—and make him guide them to the next town. This could become very abusive, so the authorities made a law that no soldier could force a citizen to guide him more than one mile. After that he had to let the first man go and pick up somebody else.

People infringe on my time in various ways. I have often thought, after someone called me up during my favorite television program and talked for half

an hour, that what I should do is call back during
his favorite program and talk another half hour,
just to go the other mile!

Let's face it: We hear these texts without paying
any attention to them. I have heard people joke a
lot about "turning the other cheek," but I've never
seen it done.

If we confront this Word of the Lord, then, we
realize that either we don't understand what the
Lord is saying, or we don't really accept it.

Fine. That brings us to step two.

2) *Asking questions*

We ask ourselves: What did Jesus really mean when
he said this? What should I really be doing if I
accept it? Such questioning helps us keep in mind
a very fundamental principle: Jesus is *not giving us
rules to follow* in the Gospels; he is giving us *examples of how he thinks*.

If we try to understand the Gospels as rules, we
immediately run into the ridiculous. Does this text
mean just what it says, so that the rule only applies
if someone wants to sue you for your coat? Or
does it mean we should never go to court with anybody, no matter what they want to take away
from us? If Jesus was just talking about coats and
shirts, the rule is too easy. If he was talking about
everything, it is impossible.

The same is true about the other mile and the other
cheek. I think I can commit myself to walking an

extra mile with a Roman soldier, if I should ever run into one who asks me. But I know I can't give everybody twice as much time as they ask for.

If we are making these texts into rules, Jesus is either asking too little, or he is asking too much. Either way it's not very practical.

But if we take these examples for what they are— *examples*—we begin to find what we were looking for in the first place: a deeper understanding of the mind and heart of God. What principle, what attitude, what way of looking at the world, what value system is operating in a man who would say what we have just heard Jesus say? What is he trying to get across to us?

With a little reflection you might come up with something like this. Jesus is giving us three examples of the same *general principle.* *Nothing on this earth should be more important to you than your brother's love.* Nothing except God himself. Not your money, not your time, not your sense of wounded dignity or pride.

Just suppose that no human being would ever fall out with another over *any material thing.* Suppose that whenever a disagreement began about money or property, each would say to the other, "Your friendship is worth more to me than this thing. *You* take it, and let's forget it!" What would that do to the history of the world?

What divides families? What causes friends to stop talking to each other? What starts wars? In how many cases does it come down to an argument over money? Over things. Suppose we would never let concern about *things* start an argument between us and another person?

So your husband just dropped ashes all over your new rug—for the 17th time. Your wife just folded in another fender on the car—parking "by ear" again. Our Lord would say it just gives you another chance to show that persons are more important to you than things—especially *this* person, who is more important to you than *any* thing.

What if you never made another person feel that your *time* is more important to you than he is? What priorities do you reveal when a person at work makes a mistake it takes you three hours of good time to rectify? When your husband leaves a ring in the tub as he goes off to work?

I went to school with a girl whose husband did that— one time too many. She went out into the yard, filled a wheelbarrow full of sand, pushed it into the bathroom and filled the tub up with sand to the level of the ring he had left. Then she packed her things, left the house, and never came back.

Most times when two people start shouting at each other, it is because they have tried to say something *too briefly*. Instead of patiently sitting down and explaining what we mean, or how we feel, we try to get the point across quicker by shouting. At that point we prefer getting results—and getting them quick—to maintaining our relationship with another person. It would be better to take the time and "walk another mile"—to talk things over before you make the short remark. In the long run, short remarks are no shortcut.

This doesn't apply to emergencies, of course. I remember a friend of mine in Texas who began methodically explaining to another just why it would not be advisable for him to keep standing in that particular spot behind that particular mule. As it happened, the mule got the point across before my friend did, and much more forcefully. The more loving thing would have been to shout.

When it comes to hurt feelings we meet the hardest challenge of all. To "turn the other cheek" doesn't seem to refer to self-defense. Our Lord is talking about a slap, and no one who really wants to attack you is going to *slap* you. He will use his fist, or a club, or a knife. (Besides, as Scripture scholars point out, the blow came on the *right* cheek, which means the other fellow was probably using the *back* of his hand assuming he was right-handed!)

To be slapped in the face is an insult, pure and simple. And Our Lord is saying that the *love* you have for your fellow man should make you willing to endure any insult, *and come back for more*, rather than break off your relationship with him!

You are walking down the hall and you smile at someone, just to be friendly. Maybe it is a new person on the job; maybe someone who looks a little down. And you get ignored, or coldly stared at. So what do you do? Most of us pull back into our armor and drop the visor down. If we stick out our neck once and get it chopped off, we don't stick it out again.

Jesus teaches we should place more value on loving our neighbor than on protecting ourselves from hurt feelings.

How many marriages have known years of grief, and perhaps ended in defeat, just because the partners were unable to get up after a hurt and risk being hurt again? How many individuals, and countries, have turned to violence because they didn't have the humility, or the love, to come back and talk again after a rebuff?

Remember, we are not speaking here about *rules*. Are there times when a person must go to court to defend his property? Yes. Should you *never* say anything to a person who is infringing on your time? No. (If you don't, you will soon have no time left.) Do you keep holding out your hand forever to someone who refuses to shake?

A rule tells you a specific thing to do. A principle shows you a general way to think. In this case, the principle is to value other people, and relationship with them, over any material thing as such, over our time as such, over our feelings of hurt and rejection as such.

Anyone can think up a whole list of situations in which we ought to protect our property, our time, our reputation. But there is never a case when a person should *prefer* his property as such to the love of another person, prefer his time over what he can do and be for people, or prefer to nurse hurt feelings when there is a possibility he can reestablish a relationship in love.

This is a revelation of God's attitude. It is not an attitude spontaneous to human beings. If an attitude like this actually became common currency in our world, our whole experience of life on this planet would be revolutionized.

Jesus is *news*. The gospel is *good* news because it tells about a man who actually thought and acted in this revolutionary way. But nothing is news just because it is written down somewhere, because one man once lived this way. News is about reality, about happenings today—right now. The gospel cannot be news to the world we live in unless there are people today who think and act as Jesus did.

We know the story of Jesus, or think we do. But we don't know what the *people who think like Jesus* are liable to come up with next. Anyone who lives by the principles of Christ is going to be news, and make news, in any age. Those who truly live by the Word of Christ—pray over it, ponder it and surrender to its spirit—do not act alone: Jesus acts in them. And Jesus will always be news, because he is always in this world as one who comes from above with a truth the world has never been able to comprehend.

I have developed above an extended reflection on one Scripture text to show how it can be done. But when you start reflecting on Scripture yourself, you might find you're not getting anywhere. Here are two more suggestions that might be helpful:

• *Ask a set of questions* that you have gotten together beforehand. A person trying to open a lock tries one key after another; if he has a whole ring of them, chances are one will work. My father taught me a little verse from the poet Rudyard Kipling that I have found helpful:

> I keep six honest serving-men;
>   (They taught me all I ever knew);
> Their names are *What* and *Where* and *When*
>   And *How* and *Why* and *Who*.

• *Try to remember other passages* in Scripture that speak to the same subject. See if they throw light on the present text or give you an idea. Some people look up parallel texts in the other Gospels. (Most Bibles give these either in the margin or in footnotes.) Other people use what is called the "topical Bible"—a book that gives all the passages in Scripture that deal with a particular topic. I personally find the *Dictionary of Biblical Theology* (edited by Father Xavier Leon-Dufour, S.J.) the most helpful book I know for meditating on different themes in the Scripture. Your actual prayer time is not usually the best time for looking up other texts or reading about a theme. But if you have done a little of this beforehand, you may remember something very useful while you are reflecting during your prayer.

3) *Taking a stance*

Constantly bear in mind that the purpose of all our reflection is to bring us to something we can respond to with our will. Above we defined the prayer of encounter as "reflecting on the word of God until we come to decisions that change our lives." Probably the most important word in this definition is *until*.

Reflecting on Scripture is not, in itself, prayer. It is prayer only if we have the intention of reflecting *until* we come to some decisions that change our life. Without this intention our reflection is not going to bring us into any real relationship with Christ.

To reflect on Scripture without letting it call our life into question is a very dangerous thing to do. That is why theologians sometimes lose their faith: They study the Scriptures so often without praying over them that, little by little, they may forget that God is speaking to their own souls through the words they are reading. To read the Scriptures "without recognizing the Lord" is to forget—and implicitly deny—that they are the word and voice of the Lord. St. Paul's warning concerning the Eucharist also applies to reading Scripture: "He who eats and drinks without recognizing the body [of the Lord] eats and drinks a judgment on himself" (1 Cor 11:29).

And so the most important stage of our prayer is the stage during which we *take a stance with our wills* toward what we have read, reflected upon and understood.

The response we make with our wills in prayer can be either *affective* or *effective*. The essential requirement of affective response is that it should be honest; of effective response that it should be concrete.

Affective response just means approval—real, honest admiration and acceptance of something the Lord has said or done. When our will responds affectively, we *desire* to be what the Lord has held out to us; we accept what he has proposed as an ideal.

The essential here is that we be *honest*. It is all right to say to Jesus, "I do believe! Help my lack of trust" (Mk 9:24). If we find it hard to accept something the Lord says, we should tell him so. We are not saying he is wrong, just that we are still sinners. It is better to stand before the Lord in the honest stance of a sinner, of one who is blind and asks for light, than to pretend to ourselves and to him that we see when we don't. "If you were blind there would be no sin in that. 'But we see,' you say, and your sin remains" (Jn 9:41).

The same is true with regard to what we see but can't do. I know, for example, that I am not able to live by the principle I myself have explained in this chapter: to never let concern for property, time or feelings take precedence over relationship with others. I see it. I agree with it. I just can't *do* it.

So I say to the Lord, "Have mercy on me, a sinner." And that is the affective response of my will to that particular teaching of the Lord.

Of course, I also have to *try* to live by what I admire in the measure that I can. I am not up to bouncing back when someone has hurt my feelings with words that are like a slap in the face. But I can turn the other cheek a *little* bit if I've just been flicked lightly on the nose. I'm not ready to walk another mile with you on a busy day, but I'm learning to take the time to dismiss people graciously.

If there is no effort at all to turn affective response into effective response, then my response is not sincere. Affective response is *desire*, not wishful thinking.

Effective response means deciding to actually *do* something. Desire becomes effective when it reaches the point of decision.

Here the essential point is that the decision be *concrete*. Man lives in time and space; he can only act in time and space. A decision to "pray more," for example, is not a decision at all. To be a decision it has to be concrete: *When* will you pray? *Where* will you pray? *How* will you pray?

If a man says, "I will say the rosary at 7:13 p.m. in the garage," that's a decision. That he can go out and do. But no man can just go out and "pray more."

A good way to get the distinction between affective and effective response—between an ideal and a resolution—is to put it into football terminology. An ideal (affective response) is like the goal line. A resolution (effective response) is like a play you call in the huddle.

To run a play well you have to be filled with desire to get across that goal line. No resolution is going to work unless a person is fired up by the ideal.

That is why it is good to spend some time in prayer just "wishing"—just looking at the ideal the Lord holds up, letting your heart go out to it, desiring to be like that, admiring the beauty of this ideal made flesh in Jesus himself. This is called *affective prayer*, and the more of it we do the better.

But no one ever made points just gazing at the goal line. If our affective prayer is authentic—if we sincerely admire what we see in Jesus and want to be like him—we will begin to call a few plays.

A play is a means to an end. The goal line is the place you want to get to, but between you and it there are a few obstacles to overcome—like the eleven movable Alps that make up the opposing team. You can't just pick up the ball and start walking.

So in the huddle the quarterback does not say, "Joe, you take the ball and make a touchdown." He has to decide whether to pass or run, whether to go around right end, left end or through the line, and so on.

Sometimes a play doesn't even aim at a touchdown; its only purpose is to pick up a few yards for a first down. In some cases it doesn't aim at any forward progress at all, but only to get the ball into a better position for a field goal or to make some yardage later on.

In other words, an ideal is *idealistic* but a resolution must be *realistic*. Ideals aim at the ideal; resolutions aim at the possible. Ideals concern what you want to *be*; resolutions concern what you can actually *do*. When we make unrealistic resolutions we get discouraged. We are aiming too high. Rather than give up, we need to aim a little lower. We should resolve to do something we *can* do right now that will help us build up to what we can't do. Everyone has a starting point; we just have to keep testing our strength until we find it.

Ready to Solo?

We have spent a good deal of time describing a basic method of prayer. We have called it the prayer of encounter. But its technical name is *discursive meditation*, and it falls into the general category of "mental prayer." Several methods exist to teach a person how to do it, but they all come down to pretty much the same thing: using our adult, spiritual powers of *memory*, *intellect* and *will*.

• With our memory we *confront*. We remember something or we read something. (Books are just the recorded memory of man.)

• With our intellect we *ask questions* and *make connections* between the old and the new; between what we are seeing now and what we have already experienced; between the person of Christ and our own experience of living as free, self-determining persons.

• With our will we *take a stance*, both affective and effective. We embrace ideals and we make resolutions.

And now you have to ask about the stance you are

taking right now: the response you are making with your will to this book. Do you intend to pray?

The ideal is beautiful: To become a "man of prayer" or a "woman of prayer." To know Jesus. To encounter the Lord. To be a Christian who has experienced the Good News and can bear witness to what he has seen and heard and touched with his own heart of the Word of Life.

> This is what we proclaim to you:
> what was from the beginning,
> what we have heard,
> what we have seen with our eyes,
> what we have looked upon
> and our hands have touched —
> we speak of the word of life.
> (1 Jn 1:1)

But does the ideal mean enough so that you will make a decision? Are you going to pray?

If you are, you need to make some decisions:
1) the *Bible* you will use (recommended editions: *The New American Bible*, *The Jerusalem Bible*, the *Revised Standard Version*);
2) the *time* you will give to prayer (when? how long?);
3) the *place* you can use for your prayer;
4) whether you are ready to do it *by yourself*.

If you don't think you're ready to solo yet, look for someone who can give you some support. This might be a friend (if you are married, ideally, your spouse) who will agree to start praying too. The two of you can meet to compare notes once a week and keep each other going, like jogging partners.

Or it might be a spiritual director. "Spiritual guide" might be a better title. Look for someone who has experience in prayer—a priest or a sister, perhaps, or another layperson who has been praying for some time already. Go to see this person regularly to report, to present your difficulties and discouragements with prayer, and to receive encouragement and advice.

If a group exists in your parish or neighborhood— even if it is just a discussion group on the Scriptures—that can provide encouragement also.

From this point it's up to you.

The Meaning of Christian 'Conversion'
CHAPTER FIVE: *Did You Ever Meet a Noia?*

John and Andrew asked Jesus, "Where do you live? Where can you be found?" His answer to them was "Come and see." And this is the answer he gives to us today. But how do we "come and see" the Lord?

The first step, explained in the last two chapters, is *communication* with Jesus. This involves listening, asking questions, responding. We call this the prayer of encounter, and it is the first step.

The second step is *conversion*. Every announcement of the Kingdom of God invites us to it: "When John the Baptizer made his appearance as a preacher in the desert of Judea, this was his theme: 'Reform your lives! The reign of God is at hand' "

(Mt 3:1-2). "After John's arrest, Jesus appeared in Galilee proclaiming the good news of God: 'This is the time of fulfillment. The reign of God is at hand! Reform your lives and believe in the gospel' " (Mk 1:14-15).

And we are told that those who heard Peter preach on Pentecost were "deeply shaken": "They asked Peter and the other apostles, 'What are we to do, brothers?' Peter answered: 'You must reform and be baptized, each one of you, in the name of Jesus Christ that your sins may be forgiven; then you will receive the gift of the Holy Spirit' " (Acts 2:37-38).

We experience the reality of Christ when we experience the *effect of his reality on our life*. And the first effect which real encounter with him should bring about within us is conversion.

Conversion may not mean what you think. It does not mean "changing religions," although sometimes that happens when a person is converted to Christ. Nor does it mean trying again to keep the Ten Commandments, although that might be a part of it.

What conversion really means is a *change of mind*: You change your way of thinking about something. You change your attitudes, rework your value system. It is a *change of heart*. This is what St. Paul was trying to get across when he told the Ephesians to "acquire a fresh, spiritual way of thinking" (Eph 4:23).

The Greek word for conversion is *metanoia*, which means "change of mind." The Gospel use of this term translates into English sometimes as "reform of life," sometimes as "repentance." Therefore, when the Gospel writers tell us to "repent," they are saying we should *change our minds* about something.

Unfortunately, what "repent" suggests to us is feeling sorrow for something we never wanted to do in the first place, but have fallen into again: like screaming at the kids, or blowing up at your wife, or getting drunk, or something worse. But strictly speaking, you can't "repent" of something you never approved of in the first place.

You may feel extreme sorrow for getting drunk. But you don't "change your mind"; you *never* really thought it was a good idea.

Of course real repentance—real conversion—can take place if you begin to see your drunkenness in a new light. Maybe you never actually thought it was a good thing to do—and so confessed it regularly; but you never thought it was all that bad either. Then one day you begin to realize there is no communication with your spouse and your kids seldom stay in the same room with you. You may also begin to notice they are following exactly the same pattern of escapism and irresponsibility they have seen in you all their lives. Gradually it dawns on you that you have never really appreciated how bad it is to get drunk. If the realization moves you to change your drinking habits, this would be a "conversion." You have "repented." You have experienced *metanoia*.

Real repentance, real conversion, I am afraid, is rare. As a priest, I seldom encounter it in confession. Most people who come to confession are not repenting; they are just showing concern about their faults. And sometimes they are not even concerned about their faults—only their consequences.

When real conversion, real repentance or *metanoia*, is taking place, we deeply change our mind about something. We see something in a new light. We raise the level of our ideals and consequently look down on behavior in our life that formerly seemed perfectly acceptable—or at least normal—to us. In the light of a new realization about things, we no longer excuse our way of acting on the grounds that it is "about par for the course."

Conversion can come from one of two sources: from looking *down* on sin, or from looking *up* to God.

Conversion which comes from *looking down on sin* is good—and more than likely a movement of grace in one's heart. But, *in itself*, such conversion is on the level of natural, of pagan religion. I don't mean that only pagans look down on sin! But if one's conversion is no more than this, it is not yet a *Christian* conversion, and *it is not the reform of life preached in the Gospels*.

We do not need the revelation of Jesus Christ to look down on what is evil. Every man—with or without the Good News of Christ—is obliged to do what is good and avoid what is evil. To be "converted" from what is evil all we need is common sense. For this "change of mind" we have only to think straight.

We can say the same about the Ten Commandments—most of which are just good, common moral sense. *We did not need Jesus to give us the Ten Commandments*. We had them already—from Moses. And therefore, to be converted to keeping the Ten Commandments, even if one kept them perfectly, is *not to be converted to Christianity*.

Thinking Like Jesus

We are truly converted to Christianity when we have changed our minds about our way of living and acting in this world, not because we are beginning to think *straight*, but because we are beginning to think *like Jesus Christ*. A Christian reform of life does not mean keeping the Ten Commandments; it means reshaping, reforming our lives along the lines of the attitudes and values of Christ. And these go far beyond the Ten Commandments.

The Ten Commandments are not news—and they weren't news even when Moses received them from God and gave them to the people. The Ten Commandments were a *confirmation* of what the Jews *already* knew, of what every healthy civilization or tribe already knows about right and wrong. (Healthy civilizations, like common sense, are not that common, of course, so we are not saying the Commandments aren't a great help.)

The Ten Commandments are not news because they are common sense. And nothing man can

figure out for himself is really news. But the attitudes and values of Jesus Christ are news—"yesterday, today and the same forever"—because they
are an insight into the very mind and heart of God.
This is the God who said,

> For my thoughts are not your thoughts,
>   nor are your ways my ways, says the Lord.
> As high as the heavens are above the earth,
>   so high are my ways above your ways
>   and my thoughts above your thoughts.
>   (Is 55:8-9)

In Jesus and through his word the thoughts of God
and the ways of God have been made known to us,
have drawn near to us. That is why Jesus is news
and always will be news.

A truly Christian conversion does not come, then,
from looking at sin, but from looking at Christ. It
is not a deeper insight into evil but a higher insight
into good. One discovers the beauty of a whole
new plane of values, the plane of God himself; the
values one saw before will never seem adequate
again.

St. Paul put it this way after his own conversion:
"But those things I used to consider gain, I have
now reappraised as loss in the light of Christ"
(Phil 3:7). Paul is not speaking about money and
pleasures, but about the moral uprightness he had
experienced by keeping the Law. He is not now
against morality; he is just saying that what he used
to think of as morality he now sees as being about
10 yards short of the starting point.

Paul's letter continues: "I have come to rate all as

loss in the light of the surpassing knowledge of my Lord Jesus Christ. For his sake I have forfeited everything; I have accounted all else rubbish so that Christ may be my wealth and I may be in him, not having any justice of my own, based on observance of the law. The justice I possess is that which comes through faith in Christ. It has its origin in God and is based on faith" (Phil 3:8-9).

Christian morality takes observance of the Ten Commandments for granted; they are not even the starting point. The morality we must be converted to is the morality of God himself—a way of looking at the world, at others, at oneself and at God that we could never establish for ourselves. It is a way of judging right and wrong that has its *origin in God* and is *based on faith*. (The "justice" we possess through faith in Christ is not just morality, of course. Paul is speaking here about the whole reality of grace, which embraces much more than the way one acts.)

When this kind of conversion takes place, we begin to experience a radical overturning of our whole system of values, our whole way of seeing and judging things. In the light of the "glory of God shining on the face of Christ," we realize how much in the dark we have always been (2 Cor 4:6). We begin to walk according to a new light, the light of Christ, who truly becomes for us our Way, our Truth, and our Life.

A full conversion to Christ is not just a matter of accepting this or that modification of one's ideals. It involves a whole new goal and direction in life.

When Jesus turns around and asks us, "What are you looking for?," he is talking about life itself.

Patty Hearst: A Study in "Conversion"

Take Patty Hearst, for example. I suppose we'll never know whether she was authentically "converted" to the ideals and principles of the Symbionese Liberation Army. She was kidnapped. She was brainwashed. That much we know. But did she at some point authentically convert from the heart, "change her mind" about the very foundations on which she was basing her life? Did she experience a *metanoia*? That we do not know.

I would like to assume here, just for the sake of argument, that she really did convert to the S.L.A. This is what the jury seems to have believed. If she did not, then plenty of other young people have—her captors, for example.

If Patty's conversion was real, what did it involve? Did she just get a little more concerned about the poor and decide to increase her annual contribution to charity by 10 per cent? Did she just make a resolution to stop talking disparagingly about minority groups, to stop telling ethnic jokes? No!

She gave up one of the richest fortunes in the United States; broke with her family; joined a group committed to violent revolution, terrorism and banditry; and accepted in advance to live the rest of her life as a hunted criminal on the run, with "no place to lay her head." She made a decision that changed the foundations, the goal, the style of her whole life. From that moment on everything in her life was ruled by one determining commitment. Nothing counted except the goals of the S.L.A. She could say like St. Paul, "I have forfeited everything; I have accounted all else rubbish."

Suppose that, instead of the S.L.A., some priest had gotten to Patty and convinced her that her whole direction in life was self-centered, superficial and meaningless. She was a Catholic, after all, although she was not living as one. Suppose she had been converted, not to a political ideal, but to Christ. Suppose she had called her parents to announce she was selling everything she owned, giving it to the poor and going to live in the poorest section of San Francisco to work as a witness to Christ among the disadvantaged? What would her parents have done?

My guess—although it might be unfair since I do not know her parents—is that, like most Catholic parents, they would have called their own favorite priest and asked him to talk her out of it. And the priest would have tried.

I knew a young man in Boston who wanted to spend a year in a monastery. He did not want to be a monk; only to get deeper into the spiritual life. He had it all arranged, until he was persuaded to talk to his uncle—a pastor in the suburbs. The uncle convinced the boy he should "finish college first"—which he did, and married out of the Church shortly afterwards. His uncle was a little "embarrassed" about that when I met him a year later while giving a talk to the Knights of Columbus.

"But it will be all right," he told me. "His wife comes from a nice family. Her father is a personal friend of mine. I'm sure they can get it fixed up."

If Patty Hearst had wanted to "sell everything and give it to the poor" as a way of following Christ, her fellow Christians would have tried to talk her out of it: "That's extreme, Patty." "You don't have to do that." "You could be killed." "You could be raped."

And what would this have said to her? That Jesus isn't worth it? That Christianity has nothing to offer that is worth sacrificing for, worth dying for, worth *living* for in a radical way? (By "radical" I don't mean "politically extreme." I mean the choices that engage the very roots of our life, the very roots of our existence, out of which every other choice comes as from its sources.)

What the cautious reasonableness of our Christianity says to people like Patty Hearst—and to all people, whether they recognize it or not—is that Christianity is a very incidental religion. It is icing on the cake, not a recipe for living. It is not something to get serious about.

But some other people broke into Patty's life— violently. People who took their own convictions very, very seriously. They were willing to live and die for them. And they not only challenged Patty to "give it all away"; they had already done so themselves. They had a cause they thought worth this much sacrifice. Unfortunately the cause was misguided; its inspiration hatred rather than love.

These were people who literally fit the warning given by St. Paul: "If I give everything I have to feed the poor and hand over my body to be burned, but have not love, I gain nothing" (1 Cor 13: 3). They had given up everything they had, and jeopardized their freedom for the rest of their lives, in order to feed the poor. And their bodies were burned—literally—in the shoot-out with the police later on in Los Angeles. Of course we would say— although when it comes to the human heart God alone can judge—that they had not love; so it counted for nothing. It didn't help either them or the poor. But they did have something they believed in.

And their conviction apparently persuaded Patty to reexamine the premises of her life. Whatever we may believe about her conversion, it seems certain she looked at the reality and purpose of her life as she had never looked at these before. And she was shaken.

"When they heard this [Peter's discourse], they were deeply shaken. They asked Peter and the other apostles, 'What are we to do, brothers?' Peter answered: 'You must reform your lives. . .' " (Acts 2:37-38). And so must we—radically, totally— or we have not heard the Good News.

Totally Reforming Our Lives

The point of this chapter is not that we should become political extremists or even activists. The example of Patty Hearst and the S.L.A. is chosen, not because it is an example of *political* conversion, but because it is an example of *total* conversion.

Patty's conversion, if it was in fact a conversion, touched the very roots of her life. It was a "radical" conversion, not in the political sense, but in the sense of a change of mind at the source, at the bottom, at the starting point of her value system.

We can say about her that "the axe was laid to the root of the tree"—the kind of change John the Baptist proclaimed. Only in her case neither the tree that died nor the tree that sprang up in its place had anything to do with the Kingdom of God. But her conversion was "radical" in the Latin meaning of the word: a conversion at the roots.

And because it was radical it was total. When the root changes, all the fruit is transformed. Touch the root and you affect the whole tree, from bottom to top. Her conversion was really an answer to the question, "What are you looking for?"—asked, not by God, but by the spokesmen of the S.L.A. From the moment of her conversion the vision of the S.L.A. illumined every choice she made; the values of the S.L.A. set the course for every step she took. This is what we mean by "conversion."

We are not limited to the example of political conversion to illustrate the point. St. Paul used the example of the Olympics! "You know that while all the runners in the stadium take part in the race, the award goes to one man. In that case, run so as to win! Athletes deny themselves all sorts of things. They do this to win a crown of leaves that withers, but we a crown that is imperishable" (1 Cor 9:24-25).

When a man is training for the Olympics, his whole life is ruled by one goal: winning in the games. This goal determines every choice he makes. Nothing is allowed to compete with it. It takes precedence over everything else in his life.

If Christ is not this for us, we have not met him, not responded to him as Redeemer, Lord and God.

If he is this for you—then you have *met-a-noia*!

Connecting Christianity With Life

CHAPTER SIX: *How to Get to Florida by Way of California*

The trouble with Christianity is that it's like your voter registration: If you don't use it you lose it.

One of the most sobering stories of loss of faith I know is the case of Simone de Beauvoir—writer, philosopher, pioneer in women's liberation and mistress of Jean-Paul Sartre. She was brought up an "ideal" Catholic girl. Her autobiography, *Memoirs of a Dutiful Daughter*, (Harper Colophon Books), tells of her upbringing: a devout mother who took her to Mass three times a week; daily visits to the chapel at school; reading the *Imitation of Christ*; little acts of mortification; meditation on the seven sorrows of Our Lady; a longing to be a

cloistered, Carmelite nun; a positive, loving, un-
troubled attitude of childlike confidence in God
and in his love for her.

This is one side of the coin. On the other side was
her father: an intellectual, brilliant man; charming
in conversation; attentive to his daughter. He
would hold discussions with her as with an adult.
In matters of religion he was a skeptic. Piety was
for women and children; he left Simone's religious
formation to her mother. Politics were his concern,
and literature and philosophy.

As Simone recalls in *Memoirs*: "This skepticism
did not affect me, so deeply did I feel myself pene-
trated by the presence of God. Yet Papa was always
right: how could he be mistaken about the most
obvious of all truths? Nevertheless, since my
mother, who was so pious, seemed to find Papa's
attitude quite natural, I accepted it calmly."

So, we begin to get the picture. Simone did not
grow up in a situation of conflict between belief
and unbelief, between a Christian mother and a
pagan father. She grew up in a situation of accommodation. She says: "Neither my mother nor my
teachers doubted for a moment that the Pope was
elected by the Holy Spirit; yet my father thought
His Holiness should not interfere in world affairs
and my mother agreed with him. . . . So I had to
swallow the paradox that the man chosen by God
to be his representative on earth had not to concern himself with earthly things. . . ."

Simone likewise noted that "national values" came

before "Catholic virtues," even for her pious
mother: "At an early age I was indoctrinated. . .to
make a clear distinction between God and Caesar
and to render unto each his due. All the same, it
was most disconcerting to find that Caesar always
got the better of God."

Civil Religion vs. Christianity

The real religion of Simone's home was "civil religion"—a code of conduct, an ethical paganism,
inspired not by any revelation from God (especially
not by the Gospels) but by the *accepted values of
one's society*. It is not the religion God brought *to*
the world, but a religion that is *of* the world. It
begins and ends in our presumptuous—or despair-
ing—acceptance that we should be a god unto ourselves.

At first glance Simone's mother—a Catholic—seems
to be the "good guy" and her pagan father the
"bad guy." In reality her mother was the "bad
guy." Her father, at least, was honest. He didn't
believe, so he didn't believe. But her mother lived
a constant denial of the faith she professed to hold.

Simone's mother had been educated by the nuns,
and they probably thought they had done a good
job. She was "profoundly conscious" of her respon-
sibilities as a Christian mother. As Simone says:
"She sought guidance from the Union of Christian
Mothers. . . . She regularly received Holy Communion, prayed long and fervently, and read num-
berless works of piety. Her personal conduct was
an outward expression of her deep faith: with

ready unselfishness, she devoted her entire being
to the welfare of those near and dear to her."

With one exception: She let her children grow up
"orthodox pagans" in a milieu that was, in reality,
that of civil religion. Simone's mother sold out to
the environment around her. She locked herself up
in the secret room of her heart with her religion
and left her world to the devil.

Thus Simone grew up in an atmosphere of harmo-
nious accommodation between her father and her
mother. The fact that they approached life from
radically opposite poles of reality—or thought they
did—didn't seem to affect the way they lived together. The fact that each one professed to understand the goal and purpose of human existence in a
way completely different from that of the other
did not cause any problem when it came to actually walking together. What does this mean?

Simone's mother *thought* she was just being toler-
ant: living her own beliefs personally, but not
forcing them on her husband. In fact she was doing
something else: She was *restricting religion to her
"devotional" life* and letting paganism—civil religion, the culture and customs which St. John calls
"the world"—*determine the practical direction of
her life*. "She decided that she would take the rules
of etiquette as her guide," notes Simone.

If Simone's mother really believed in Christ and
her father didn't, it should have made some difference in the direction of their individual lives. It was
as if she thought the way to the Promised Land lay
through Florida and he thought it passed through

California. But their "compromise" was that he would drive the car toward California while she sat in the back and read tourist brochures about Florida to the children!

Simone's mother apparently never saw the contradiction. After all, the civil religion, the "nice" thing to do in her society, allowed her to disapprove of overt sin. Women were even expected to disapprove. She never had to break the Ten Commandments or stop going to Mass. She probably couldn't think of anything serious to bring up in confession.

But when her daughter grew up and looked back on her life, analyzing why she had lost the Faith, she was able to put her finger on exactly what had happened: "...I grew accustomed to the idea that my intellectual life—embodied by my father—and my spiritual life—expressed by my mother—were two radically heterogeneous fields of experience which had absolutely nothing in common. . . . So I set God apart from life and the world, and this attitude was to have a profound influence on my future development."

What Simone de Beauvoir saw was the truth—the truth of her environment, the truth of her cultural milieu. It was not the truth of what religion *ought* to be, but it was the truth of her parents' understanding of religion. And it may be the truth of our own.

When you get right down to it, Simone's mother and father had the same religion. Otherwise they could not have lived together. They did not have the same *devotions*. They did not use the same *symbols* to express their basic orientation toward life. She read a prayerbook; he read the newspaper. And they *talked* about reality in different terms. But they *lived* reality according to the same basic value system.

Madame de Beauvoir's "religious values" were acceptable to others as long as they were kept discreetly out of practical affairs. They belonged to her private life, the world of daydreams and hobbies, where we are free to dream our own dreams and find solace in the symbols that appeal to our own heart.

She accepted this tolerance of her religion, and in doing so found herself—unwittingly—in perfect agreement with that understanding of religion which her husband had held all along: Religion is a matter of one's personal feeling about things. It is fine for those who need it; but you would not expect intelligent, practically-oriented people to have time for it. To practice religion is to take "time out" occasionally to acknowledge one's theoretical dependence on God before plunging back into the *real* business of making a living in this world. Religion is for those who get turned on by "metaphysical" things like God. But religion has nothing significant to say about *life*.

How "Accommodating" Are We?

If we are honest with ourselves, is there any difference at all between Madame de Beauvoir's religion and our own—except that she was a little more fervent on the devotional side? Can we name anything in our practical lives (what Simone de Beauvoir calls the sphere of "human things—culture, politics, business, manners, and customs") which makes us a rock of contradiction to anyone who is not a convinced Christian?

Let's take a look at some "little" things first. Rather than starting with the joists and foundation stones of our lives, let's begin by looking at the paint job and the trimmings.

Do we "accommodate" to the language of the world? We would not tolerate anyone's using the name of our wife for profanity. Why is it "not the same" when someone claims the freedom to curse with the name of the God we adore?

The *culture* we live in understands and approves of a man who takes respect for his wife's name seriously. But our *culture* does not understand or approve of a man who takes respect for God's name seriously unless this is confined to the privacy of his own heart. Family values are part of our civil religion; Christian values are not.

A man who is serious about racial equality would not dream of letting a word like *nigger* go unchallenged. But the same man, professing to be a serious Christian, would not challenge an associate who used the name of God profanely. Public disrespect for minority groups violates our civil religion; public disrespect for God does not.

On the other hand, the civil religion does not demand that we treat black people as our brothers. Yet Christianity says they are our brothers; it says this in a quite literal sense about *anyone* who has been reborn in grace as a child of God, who can say to God, "Our Father." But if our friends find black people unacceptable at a party or a dance, we manage diplomatically not to invite black people.

We accept the rules of the civil religion: Black people can be our brothers in a *religious* sense, provided we do not present them to others as our brothers in a *social* sense. In other words, we can *say* they are our brothers so long as we do not *act* as if they are. Religion is acceptable so long as it does not interfere with the way people *live*.

Personally, we can hold sex to be as sacred as we like, and we can be as strict about it in our private lives as we care to be—the civil religion grants us this right. But it is not socially acceptable to be sticky about dirty jokes, sexy clothes or pornographic pictures in the public sphere, especially if we're talking about high-class porn like *Playboy*. The civil religion has gotten around to protecting citizens from exposure to tobacco smoke in airplanes (our culture respects arguments that have to do with health), but it does not recognize a person's right to be free from unsolicited sexual provocation in public places, unless this takes a very extreme form.

You can ask the neighbor's daughter to leave your house if she is soliciting the guests. But you can't ask her to stay away from your swimming pool if she's wearing a bikini, because "everybody else" is doing it. A prude is defined as one whose attitude toward sex is less permissive than the culture's. No one would dream of asking whether a bikini expresses a Christian respect for woman; the only question is whether the civil religion—current etiquette—allows it.

Civil religion is simply another name for paganism. It is what "nice" people in one's society do—what the culture approves of. Simone de Beauvoir's father had civil religion, although he did not believe in God. (This actually makes him an atheist, which good pagans are not). So did Simone's mother, although she did not know or admit it.

And so, quite possibly, do we.

What value system does *our* dress express? Our language? Our circle of friends? The car we drive? The stores we buy in? The food we put on the table? The neighborhood we have chosen to live in? The work we do to make a living? The place we go for our vacation? The political party we support? The magazines we bring into our house? The way we budget our money? The way we allocate our time?

It is not these details *as such* that we are concerned about. There is no identifiably "Christian" way to dress, speak, drive, eat. There are no specifically "Christian" jobs in the marketplace as opposed to non-Christian jobs. Jesus made no *rules* about these things.

What is important is not specifically *how* one eats, drinks, dresses, drives, works and so on, but *how one decides how*.

You cannot identify a contestant in the Olympics by what he eats. At Montreal in 1976 one contestant began his day with four large steaks for breakfast; another with just six strawberries. But one thing you can be sure of: Each contestant *chooses* what to eat with only one guiding principle in mind: What will help to win in the games? A serious athlete does not eat whatever is served just because it is polite, or because everybody else is eating it, or because he or she has been brought up on it.

So you can't identify Christians by any one way of eating, drinking, dressing, etc. But you *should* be able to identify Christians by the obvious fact that they clearly eat, drink and do everything for the glory of God. They are guided by a desire to live completely, totally, by the gospel of Jesus Christ. They are not people who "fit in." Their way of acting will be *news*.

Becoming Christian Nonconformists

Christians do not set out to be nonconformists. But their whole life is guided—in practice and not just in theory—by a vision of the world, a set of values that do not conform with the seeing and thinking of this world.

When Christians are *not* nonconformists, they realize, sooner or later, that their belief is not real, that God does not really exist for them—not the Christian God, at least.

For Simone de Beauvoir the moment of truth came early—around the time of adolescence. She had been going to confession regularly twice a month for seven years to the same priest. She would accuse herself of all the things "religion" was concerned with: lack of fervor at Holy Communion, distractions during prayer, of not thinking often enough of God during the day. At the same time she had begun to do a lot of things that never came up in confession: They had nothing to do with "religion." She was reading books her parents had forbidden her to read, telling lies, indulging in sexual fantasies, being insolent in class.

It may surprise us that she never thought of these things as being "sins," as having anything to do with religion or confession. But it was quite consistent with the way she had been brought up: Religion did not come into conflict with the real, the practical things of life. She read books because she had a thirst for knowledge. Her intellectual life had nothing to do with her religious life. She lied to her parents because it was the only way she could keep doing what she felt she had to do without causing a scene. And sex fascinated her. These were the things of earth; they had nothing to do with God.

She describes her religious frame of mind this way: "All nature spoke to me of God's presence. But it

seemed to me quite definitely that he was a total
stranger to the restless world of men. My insolence
in class and my furtive reading of banned books
did not concern him." This is mysticism without
morality, Christianity without conversion of life:
pure illusion.

Finally her "complacency received a nasty shock."
Someone apparently tipped off her confessor that
Simone was not quite the saint she thought she
was. He brought it up to her very gently one day
in confession: "I hear that my little Simone is
changing. . .that she is disobedient, noisy; that she
answers back to her teachers. . . . From now on
you must be on your guard against these things."

And she burned. She couldn't believe that this
priest whom she had accepted as the voice of her
mystical God could be, after all, a sin-sniffer, a
clucking nurse of the establishment. Could God be,
like this priest, so stupid, as "fussy and narrow-
minded as a church hen?"

She never went back to him in confession. She
tried a few others but it didn't work. She had had
it with priests.

Finally the moment of truth reached its climax. It
was the turning point of her life: "One evening. . .
I was leaning out of my window. . . . I had spent
my day eating forbidden apples and reading, in a
book of Balzac—also forbidden. . . . 'These are sins,'
I told myself. It was impossible to deceive myself
any longer. . . . I listened to the gurgling of the
water, and I knew then that nothing would make

me give up earthly joys. 'I no longer believe in God,' I told myself, with no great surprise. That was proof: If I had believed in him, I should not have allowed myself to offend him so light-heartedly. . . . That is why I felt so little surprise when I became aware of his absence in heaven and in my heart. I was not denying him in order to rid myself of a troublesome person: on the contrary, I realized that he was playing no further part in my life and so I concluded that he had ceased to exist for me." She was 14 years old.

To me this is one of the most terrifying passages in human literature. It is a cold, deliberate, perfectly lucid choice between God and self. It has none of the demented mania of Adolf Hitler, none of the sickening self-deception of the Pharisee. It is the frank, clear-minded decision of an adolescent girl calmly choosing life on her own terms over faith and obedience to God. From the time she made this choice until the writing of her autobiography 37 years later, she is able to testify, "My incredulity never once wavered." Her loss of faith was complete. So far as we know, it was final.

Simone de Beauvoir's life is an illustration of the rule: "When much has been given a man, much will be required of him" (Lk 12:48); and, "Whoever has will be given more, but the one who has not will lose the little he has" (Lk 19:26).

If you don't use your faith, you lose it.

Before we write Simone off as a "strange case," let's reflect a little on our own lives. Yes, we probably confess many moral failures in confession. Lies, sexual fantasies, overt stealing—it would never occur to us to leave these things out of confession. After all, they were explicitly taught to us as part of our religion.

But business practices? Racism? Breaking civil laws? Polluting the environment (throwing beer cans along the side of the highway, for example)? Toleration of an overcrowded, dehumanizing and physically dangerous prison system? Accepting the standards of our society on how much money we spend, what we spend it on, and what kind of people we associate with while we're spending it? Challenging consumerism, affluence, waste? Concern for our brothers and sisters in the underdeveloped nations? Using our time on this earth as a precious talent God has given us to invest for the Kingdom of God?

I once gave a retreat to high school girls that somehow developed into a discussion about the Christian use of money. One girl, a deep and lucid thinker, finally mused out loud: "I guess if I'm really a Christian I shouldn't buy a new dress for the Christmas dance." She paused a moment and added, "But I have to buy a new dress if I'm *going* to the Christmas dance."

There you have it in a nutshell. You can't sit in a car that's headed for California if you really want to go to Florida.

Yes, it means in a sense that Christians have to "drop out" of this world. It doesn't mean they have to leave it and go to the desert. But they have to be willing to *sacrifice everything the world has to offer* rather than compromise—in the slightest—their Christian ideals. And this means the *expression* of their Christian ideals in action.

You can go to the dance. But not to the dance "they" are giving. You go in last year's dress, and by that very fact are not playing by the rules of the game. You go to the dance on your own terms, and that makes it a different kind of dance—or makes you a very unacceptable person.

I knew some high school boys in Memphis, Tennessee, who got together and decided not to buy their dates expensive corsages for the junior-senior prom. They gave the money to the poor instead. By that very fact the prom became, for them, more than just an occasion to have fun with their own little clique by the standards of this world. It became an occasion to have fun while simultaneously expressing a Christian awareness of the *whole* reality of this world, the reality that is found outside of the make-believe boundaries and trimmed hedges of the country club.

We can say they "dropped out" of the dance that was being given; that in a very real sense they went to their own dance: The dance where they were was not where they were "at."

I don't know what their dates thought about it. But I know they *thought*. That made the boys' action "Christian witness"—an action that doesn't make sense until you explain it by the attitudes and values of Christ.

If we are going to be Christians, if we are going to *know* Jesus Christ, we are going to have to reform our lives. This doesn't mean tightening up this little laxity or that, but reshaping the whole pattern, giving a whole new direction and form to everything we do. Nothing else is worthy of God. Nothing else is worthy of the name *religion*.

Simone de Beauvoir was an "extremist," she says, because she "could not admit any kind of compromise arrangement with heaven. However little you withheld from him, it would be too much if God existed; and however little you gave him, it would be too much again if he did not exist. . . . As soon as I saw the light, I made a clean break."

To be an extremist is good. As Rabbi Heschel said, "To deal moderately with God is a profanation"—it is blasphemy. But not to *judge* moderately of *oneself* is blasphemy again; it is pride. We cannot respond totally to the Master overnight. We can only accept our sinfulness, our selfishness, our blindness with humility and sit at his feet as disciples. He will gradually lead us to the total gift of ourselves.

But the disciple must accept, from the beginning, that his whole life *is going* to change. This is how it must be if one is dealing with God. This is how it must be with us.

We should be able to identify clearly the effect that the person and example of Jesus Christ is having on our lives. If that effect is not all-embracing and "radical"—touching the very *roots* of our existence—then we will have to face the fact, sooner or later, that we have never truly encountered him, that he is not "real" to us.

Let us hope that does not take place on Judgment Day.

The Support of a Community of Faith
CHAPTER SEVEN: *Two for the High Board*

In previous chapters we have talked about the first
two steps necessary in an attempt to encounter
Christ: *communication* through prayer and *conversion*. Now we take up the third element that must
be involved in any authentic response to Jesus'
invitation, "Come and see": *Christian community*.

We don't mean that community is the last of these
elements in a chronological sense. Any one of the
three—prayer, conversion or community—might
come first, second or third in the order of time.
But all three have to be "realized" in a person's
life for encounter with Christ to be true and complete

Instead of starting with a definition of "Christian community," we will build up to it. Let's begin with the scene at the Jordan again, when John and Andrew encountered Christ. What got them going? What started them down the road to follow him?

Was it the preaching of John the Baptist?

Not really. John's preaching prepared them, of course. John's preaching pointed Jesus out. But the first time John pointed to Jesus as the "Lamb of God" nobody moved. Why?

It was too much for them. It was unexpected. It was just a bigger leap than anyone was prepared to make. They couldn't respond.

What really got John and Andrew started was *community*. John looked at Andrew; Andrew looked at John; and they said, "Let's go." That's community.

Remember the first time you dove off the high board as a kid? What got you going? Did you go to a pool all by yourself, look at that diving board way up in the air, and respond in solitary courage to the challenge of it?

Or did some other kid say, "I'll jump if you will"?

Perfectly illogical, of course. If it's too high for one person, it's too high for two. And the fact that some other kid's body is going to splatter on the water next to yours doesn't help your case at all.

But we *need* that other person before we'll jump.

This is why we need community in the faith—why we need *faith-community*. It is always—and always will be—"too big a leap" to do the things of God alone. There have been saints and heroes who have done it: They are the prophets *par excellence*. They are the ones who can live by the principle my father once taught me: "The eagle flies alone."

All of us are not eagles. Although all of us must fly alone sometimes. Like Johnathan Livingston Seagull we have to *learn* to leave the flock, if God calls us to soar that high. But we first learn our soaring *in* the flock. We need a lot of support to take that first leap off familiar ground. And we need support to keep entrusting ourselves to the apparent insolidity of the air until we acquire a "feel" for flying. Once flying is in our blood, we can then soar alone.

Did you ever observe the phenomenon of three logs in a fire? Put them together, and they will burn brightly. Separate them from one another, and the fire begins to go out.

Why should this be? It is a law of mathematics that the whole is not greater than the sum of its parts. If each log is on fire, if each has reached its combustion point, why should each not continue to burn until it is consumed, with or without the others? Why should there be more fire, more heat, more light, from several logs burning together than from the same number burning separately?

But there is.

Logs are like people. To spend themselves becoming light and heat, to keep going beyond their natural state, they need a little help from their friends. Then they can transcend themselves; they can be fire on earth.

It is not natural to man to burn with the brightness of God. He is capable, through grace, of thinking God's thoughts, of following God's ways. But it is God himself who said,

For my thoughts are not your thoughts,
nor are your ways my ways, . . .
(Is 55:8)

When we try thinking and acting "like God," it never feels completely "natural." We are always subject to that nagging question, "Is this really real? Am I out of my head? I must be crazy to act this way!"

It is very hard for us to leave the beaten path.

Once, when I was a missionary in Africa, we lost a herd of cattle bought to teach the people in our villages how to plow. A young herdsman hired to watch the cows fell asleep one Sunday, and when he woke up the cows were gone.

On horseback I went after them, down a trail I had never followed before. I knew the trail ran parallel to a creek and that a few miles farther down it crossed a road. There was "no way" I could get lost.

But I did, of course. I lost the trail, lost my sense of direction, and pretty soon just tied up the horse in a clearing and sat down to wait for the moon to come up.

I knew the moon always rose in the east—until it came up in what I was prepared to swear *had* to be the west. My first inclination was to call the laws of nature into question. "Maybe the moon rises in the west *sometimes*," I thought. Then I saw the Southern Cross—a constellation only visible near the tropics—which is always found toward the south. It was in the north!

I was still hesitating when a sound of something stirring around in the bush behind me activated my decision-making capacity in marvelous fashion. If the moon really rose in the east, and the Southern Cross really stayed in the south—*and* if there really was something out there rustling around in the leaves—then the best way for me to go was to my left, where the creek had to be. I could follow the creek to the road and be home before sunrise.

I started off to the left. Soon I ran into a little wisp of a path. It didn't look very promising, but it did look like a path—even though it was going in the wrong direction.

Would you believe I turned and followed it? I turned away from what I knew was the right direction and started going down that path—reflecting to myself as I did so: "Now isn't that human nature? We would rather follow the beaten path in what we *know* is the wrong direction, than launch out in the right direction all by ourselves without a path."

Fortunately my wisp of a path petered out almost immediately, and I turned back again toward the creek, found my road and lived happily ever after.

This is human nature. We don't follow what *we* know to be true; we follow what we see *other people* doing. This is not because we are indecisive, wishy-washy people. We just find it very difficult to believe that we could be the *only* one right when everybody else is doing something different.

Were you ever the only person in a singing group who hit the right note when everyone else was flat? Were you able to hold the true note?

Community Shapes Our Belief

When I was a student in Catholic high school, we were taught that segregation was wrong—by the teachers in our segregated school. We naturally asked why, then, we had not integrated. (This was before the 1954 Supreme Court decision abolishing the "separate but equal" principle that allowed state-enforced segregation. Segregation was still the law, and integration was illegal in our state.) We were told it was better to be a segregated school and stay open than to defy the law and not to be a school at all. We were taught, in other words, that it is better to follow the civil religion and deny the gospel *in action* than to be a martyr and lose the right to teach Christianity *in theory*.

How could we have been so blind?

It was easy. We weren't blind; we were just looking in the same direction everyone else was looking.

And when everyone looks in the same direction, it is easy for a lot of reality to pass unnoticed. It usually takes a loud crash somewhere to make people turn around.

A faith-vision is always in opposition to the overall worldview of the culture. That is why faith and prophecy go together.

But sometimes on some particular issue the direction in which faith looks and the direction in which the culture looks seem to coincide. They don't exactly coincide. Rather, faith and the culture, each looking in its own direction, get a particular issue in focus at the same time and they crisscross. Then a person finds faith and culture both encouraging the same moral choice.

That makes things easy in the short run, but it is very dangerous for religion—at least for Christianity—in the long run. It can lead Christians to believe they are acting according to their faith-vision when in reality they are just conforming to their culture. Catholics are not integrating their schools today because their faith made them prophetic. They are integrating because the culture has finally made integration a commandment of the civil religion. Catholics are now glad to cooperate because their own religion has been telling them all along that they should have been integrated in the first place.

That is to say, our religion has been telling us this *in theory*. *In practice*, our faith-community was teaching us just the opposite. How could we accept segregation all those years when it was in such glaring opposition to the gospel? How could Christians accept slavery for so many centuries? Or the Inquisition? Or systematic persecution of the Jews in the name of Jesus of Nazareth, King of the Jews?

We accepted these things because everyone did—*including those in the community of the faith.* Catholics built and conducted segregated schools as if nothing were wrong with it. Catholics bought and owned slaves and sold them like property to the highest bidder when they chose to. Catholics persecuted the Jews and tortured the prisoners of the Inquisition. (We console ourselves by saying that Protestants were just as bad!)

It was not just the culture that was shortsighted or cross-eyed on these issues. It was the community of believers.

But *in theory* the "Church" was teaching, as she always had, the doctrine of Jesus Christ. She was standing by the riverbank like John the Baptist saying, "There goes the Lamb of God." It was from the Church—from our own religious teachers—that we learned in high school that segregation was wrong. And it was from the Church—the community of believers, including those same religious teachers—that we learned it was all right to do nothing about it!

The Church proclaimed to us, "There goes the Lamb of God," and nobody followed him, including those who were pointing him out. If some members of the congregation did rise to follow Jesus, it was as if a voice from the crowd said, "Sit down!" Since everybody else was sitting down, and since even the Church people pointing Jesus out didn't move themselves, the congregation concluded they weren't supposed to take literally what John—and the Church—said. So they sat down.

I don't want to appear too hard on my religious teachers. The focus at this point is on what we *failed* to do for one another as a community. If I started to describe how the men and women who taught me succeeded, by their example, in introducing me to the person of Jesus Christ in grade school and high school, I would never have time to finish. If I make it to heaven I owe it—after my father and mother—to the Daughters of Charity and the Jesuits.

But when everyone is *looking* the same direction *in action*, the fact that somebody, while looking west, is saying in a quiet tone of voice, "He's really in the east," doesn't move anybody to turn around. We just find it almost impossible to believe, in spite of the testimony of our hearts and our minds, that what everybody is actually doing is not the right thing to do. We are unable to believe it even if the others *tell us themselves* it is not the right thing to do.

Actions speak louder than words. Words hardly speak at all.

We need Christian community to support us when we begin to see what it means to follow Christ. We need this support both in order to *believe* and in order to *act* on what we believe. We can "begin to see" what it means to follow Christ without yet actually believing—fully and firmly—that we must change the way we live in order to follow him.

It is typical of faith response that it begins in great doubt and uncertainty. Take the Magi, for example. They were pagans, worshiping the God of purity, symbolized for them by fire. They sought him through the fiery bodies of the heavens, the stars. So when God wished to reveal his Son to them, he didn't send them an angel, as he did to the shepherds outside of Bethlehem. The Magi would not have known what to make of an angel. No, he spoke to them in their own language: He sent a star.

When the star came, something in their hearts responded. In one sense they knew this was something different, that God was speaking to them. And yet, when they *thought* about it, there were so many reasons for saying it was probably just another comet, a natural phenomenon. After all, astronomy is full of surprises. Just like life.

Community Encourages Us to Risk

When you think of the risks involved, it is a wonder they ever responded at all. I mean, you don't just jump on a camel and start off following a star across the desert. They had to deal with many practical questions: How long are we going to be gone? When can my wife expect me back? How much water will we have to pack on the camels?

If the star wasn't from God, they were liable to die in the desert.

Fortunately there were three of them. They could encourage each other to take the risk. And if their friends were like most people's friends, they needed all the encouragement from one another they could get. People who are not touched by the vision can give a million reasons to people who are touched why they should not respond. Our friends can be our enemies when it comes to faith response, unless they, too, have been touched by the vision of faith.

The three Wise Men were not just friends. From the moment the star shone on them all, and they began to respond, they were a *community of faith*.

To a faith community a person can bring what might be an inspiration of God and get help in discerning it. The community will have been opened by their own experience to the fact that God moves in strange ways—beautiful, risky ways. A faith community expects God to call people to walk on water. And a faith community knows it is worth the risk of walking on water *just to find out* whether the vision one sees is, in fact, Jesus or a ghost.

When Jesus came walking over the water to his apostles in the boat, they thought he was a ghost. But Peter called out, "Lord, if it is really you, tell me to come to you across the water" (Mt 14:28).

It's a wonder the apostles let Peter jump. Out of the whole boatload there apparently wasn't one with enough common sense to say, "Peter, don't be an idiot. If it *is* a ghost, what do you think he's going to say? He's going to say, 'Come!' If it's a ghost, he *wants* you to drown!"

Then Jesus said, "Come!" And Peter leaped.

When Jesus says, "Come and see!," there is often a hidden clause. It is as if he adds under his breath, ". . .at the risk of your life!"

Real response to God *is* a risk of one's life. As Jesus himself said, "Whoever would preserve his life will lose it" (Mk 8:35). But even more, *no response is worthy of God that isn't a risk of life.*

A gambler can say, "Put your money where your mouth is," because you are only gambling for money. In marriage, spouses express love with their bodies, because they have become two in one flesh. Each says to the other, "This is my body, which is given up for you." But when we respond to God—who is Life itself—the language of love must be life itself.

Abraham was on the way to becoming quite a wealthy man. His sheep were reproducing steadily and his goats were making him the cheesiest citizen in town. There was only one problem: Abraham had no children.

His wife was sterile. Abraham knew by now there weren't going to be any children. So he began reflecting on what his life would mean after he was dead.

Abraham came from a pretty primitive tribe. There wasn't any art or science to speak of, very little culture or politics. Life was mainly all about raising sheep and goats. If you wanted to stand out, to individuate yourself in the tribe, the best way—in fact, about the only way—was to raise a bigger herd of sheep and goats than the next fellow.

Abraham had done this. But when he died, what would it all mean? He had no heir, no one who bore his name. His herd would be divided up among the tribe—and with it his individuality. His life's work would be absorbed into the tribe—and so would the meaning of his life.

It was really getting to him.

Then God offered him a deal: "Go forth from the land of your kinsfolk, and from your father's house to a land that I will show you. I will make of you a great nation" (Gn 12:1). God promised ultimate meaning in life if Abraham, on his side, would leave everything that gave life meaning here and now.

The wager has to match the stakes, otherwise you don't deserve to be in the game. If Abraham wanted meaning in life, God would give him meaning in life. But Abraham would have to show—would have to *know* in his own heart—that he was taking God seriously. It's too easy to say, "Oh sure, God, you do that for me." That's not a covenant. That's not even belief.

If God was going to get himself involved with Abraham, Abraham would have to get himself involved with God. He would have to show he was really placing his stakes on God, really putting his future in God's hands, basing it on God's promise, on his word. If he trusted in God for the meaning of his life, he would have to trust in God for *all* the meaning in his life. No covering his bets. No contingency insurance.

This is the deal every time God speaks. And that is why faith and courage have to go together. It isn't enough to believe in some abstract, verbal way. When God asks for faith, he asks for *proof* that we believe. And this proof takes the form of risk:

"Follow the star."

"Walk on the water."

"Leave."

There are a few, like Abraham, who can just leave everything and walk out into the desert, trusting in God. But most of us don't have the courage.

And so we need community. We need other believers, not only to confirm our belief that God is speaking to us, but to give us the courage to act upon it.

It's like diving off the high board: "I'll jump if you will."

"I'll go out into the desert if you will."

"I'll sell everything I have and give it to the poor if you will."

"Let's follow the Lord!"

How Faith Community Happens

CHAPTER EIGHT: *Anyone Got a Barley Loaf?*

We need the support of faith community if we are to follow the Lord. This community might be a parish, a family, a husband or wife, a prayer group, a friend. Anytime there are two or three gathered together in his name, it is a community of faith—*if* they are truly gathered in his name.

To be gathered *in* his name is not the same as to be gathered *under* his name—to be called "Christian," or "The Catholic Whatchamacallit Guild," or the "Saint Whoosis Parish Thingamajig Society." In fact, we can question whether most groups gathered together *under* the name of Christ are gathered *in* his name at all.

Not that they are gathered for anything bad. It is just that the *name*, the *person* of Jesus Christ is seldom our real focus. Our attention and efforts are usually focused on something else: a liturgy to "put on" or to "get through," depending on our measure of participation; a sermon to deliver, to hear; a parish bazaar to organize; a building to pay for; a recreational program to provide; a social; a school; Thanksgiving baskets for the poor; a lynching party for the pastor.

We have spoken (see Chapter 1) about the image Catholics project of their expectations at Mass. By and large we appear to have a "code and cult" mentality. We come to hear a sermon that will give us a push, or a little more courage, to keep the rules as we already understand them. And we come to "fulfill our obligation" to attend Mass. To judge from the singing, very few come with the idea of making a personal contribution.

Ask a Catholic if he made a "contribution" at Mass and he'll tell you how much he put in the collection plate! Ask him, "How was the Mass?," and he'll talk about the sermon, or the singing (someone else's), or whether the priest declaimed or droned. For many of us the Mass is a spectator sport. We expect to be "turned on" or "turned off," but we are determined to keep going in any case because a law is a law.

What Catholics seldom talk about is what *Jesus* did at Mass—how they experienced *him*, what *he* did in and through the congregation gathered in his name; how they came "to know him in the breaking of the bread" (Lk 24:35). But Jesus actually promised, "Where two or three are gathered in my name, there am I in their midst" (Mt 18:20).

And he was—quite experientially—in the early Church's assemblies. St. Paul, writing to the Galatians, is able to appeal to their *experience of Christ present and acting through his Spirit* as a basis to prove a theological point: "*How did you receive the Spirit*? Was it through observance of the law? Or through *faith in what you heard*?. . . Is it because you observe the law, or because you have faith in what you heard that God lavishes the Spirit on you and works wonders in your midst?" (Gal 3: 2, 5; emphases added).

In other words, what gave the first Christians their sense of unity when they gathered together was not that they could look to the folks on either side of them and be reassured by their obvious commitment to the rules. The Mass was not a vote of confidence in the established order of things, a sort of body count for the law-and-order party in the Church.

It was an experience of *God present and acting* in and through the congregation gathered there. The Mass was a spiritual experience, an experience of Christ.

The Acts of the Apostles and the letters of St. Paul and the other apostles usually speak of this as being an experience of the Holy Spirit. The best explanation I know of this experience of the Holy Spirit is given by Father John Haughey, S.J., in *The Con-*

spiracy of God (Doubleday, 1973). I will cite just a couple of his thoughts:

The "experience of the Holy Spirit," he says, is more an experience of *knowing Jesus and the Father through the action of the Holy Spirit* than an experience of the Spirit as such: "The Spirit aims at being inconspicuous. In activity it points to the Other, making us aware of Jesus as our Lord and God as our Father."

This is not just an academic awareness of Jesus as an historical fact or a theological reality. Through the action of the Spirit in our hearts and within the community we become aware of Jesus as a *living*, *present person* standing in our midst today. The Father and the Son send the Spirit to us, and through their Spirit are present to us in a living way themselves.

"Without the Spirit," Haughey says, "Jesus would have been to Christians only a model, a goal, a memory, an ideal. But given the personality of the Spirit, Jesus has become Emmanuel, God-with-us. Because of the Spirit it is possible for the Senders— Jesus and the Father—to join the Sent."

As a result, people touched by the Spirit are *able to bear witness*. Their witness is not so much to the Spirit as such, *but to Jesus*. They "know the Lord" and can proclaim to others what they have "seen with their eyes, and heard with their ears, and touched with their hands of the Word of life."

"The result of the Spirit's touch," in Haughey's words, "is a consciousness-raising, not a conscious-

ness of the Spirit as such, but a profound awareness of and capacity to witness to Jesus and his
Father, and to love the self that is the recipient of
such love."

One proof we have experienced the reality of God's
love is that we *love ourselves*. There is a newfound
peace, confidence, joy, self-acceptance and security
that comes from our interior realization of being
accepted and loved by the Father, of being recon-
ciled and redeemed by the Son.

If we have experienced God's love, if we have realized what and who Jesus Christ is for us, it will *not
be possible for us to remain silent*. We will witness—
more by our actions than by our words, but inevitably by both. As Haughey puts it: "We inevitably
point to where our hearts are by the things we say
and do."

Haughey's conclusion is this: "The massive, general reluctance of the majority of Christians even
to point to or confess God's love of them to others
suggests that they have yet to receive the Power
they need to become what they already are in
God's eyes and do the work of loving in his name."

So where do we start? We begin with prayer and
conversion of our own lives, of course. We can only
witness to what we have known. And we have only
truly known that which has in some real way transformed our lives.

But in order for us to become *aware* of what we
have in fact seen and known we may need to begin
with some experiences of sharing the faith in com-

munity. And for some it may take an experience in community before they can even begin to "come and see" through prayer and personal conversion of life.

Let us look, then, at what a *Christian community* really is.

Making the Lord Present

A community is a group of people with a *common unity*. They may have a common unity of *past experience*, something they have been through together that has given them a special appreciation for one another: the survivors of a shipwreck, for example; or the members of a victorious Olympic team. Families have this kind of unity; they have lived through a lot together. So do the alumni who show up for a class reunion. The citizens of a country have it; that is one reason why the nation's history is taught in school—to let the young participate in the shared past experience of the nation and, thus, become members of the community.

To really have life, though, the community must also have a common *future*. The members must have a common unity of *purpose*. There must be something they are *trying to do together*.

To the extent that this common purpose means a lot to each member, each member will mean a lot to every other member. When working for a goal or a cause you really believe in, the presence of another person who believes in it as strongly as you do is a great support. You begin to appreciate that person very much. You discover more and more things you have in common: similar points of view, similar experiences and turning-points in your lives. You realize you have thought the same thoughts, felt the same things, adopted the same desires. You know you can count on one another. You become very precious to each other.

A Christian community is a group of people with a shared past *and* a common future. They *have known* the Lord through faith, and they *are seeking together to know* the Lord more fully and to make him known to the world. They are witnesses and they are disciples.

I like this definition of Christian community: a group of people who come together to remember the Lord and, by remembering, to make him present.

A Christian community can make the Lord present in two ways: in worship and celebration, in conversation and prayer that "remembers the Lord"; or in a way of living and working in this world that is inexplicable except through the power of the Spirit of Christ acting through faith, hope and love.

We will look at the first of these, worship, in the remainder of this chapter and at the second in Chapter 9.

The prototype, the model and ideal, of Christian community actively making the Lord present through worship is the *Mass*. The Mass was inaugurated at the Last Supper when Jesus took bread, gave thanks to the Father, broke the bread and gave it to his disciples, saying: "This is my Body, to be given for you. Do this as a remembrance of me" (Lk 22:19).

The Mass, then, is a way of "remembering the Lord." And in this remembrance the Lord becomes present in three ways: through his Word, through his Spirit in the Mystical Body, and through the Eucharist.

Jesus' Presence in His Word

The Mass is scriptural, of course, from beginning to end. But the first part of the Mass, the part we call the Liturgy of the Word, is essentially a prayer service centered on reading and responding to the Scriptures.

Reading the Scripture at Mass is not quite the same as reading the Scripture at home (and neither can substitute for the other). At Mass the Scripture is *proclaimed*—that is, it is read out loud to all the people as the public expression of the truth all hold in common. And Jesus is present addressing his people through his proclaimed Word. (At home each person meditates and prays over Scripture in private and Jesus speaks to each in his heart.)

The very fact of a *listening* congregation at Mass bears witness to the Lord's presence. It is a visible, public manifestation of faith in the reality of Jesus speaking to his people through his Word.

Then the Scriptures are explained. In the homily the speaker interprets the Scripture in the name of the whole community. In the homily Christ's words are put into the context of the present day. They are examined in light of their application to current events, to the reality of persons' lives here and now. The timeless Word of God is made timely. Jesus lives still through his Word.

Already in the homily we also have Christ becoming present in another way: not only through the Scripture, but also through the Holy Spirit speaking in a member of Christ's Mystical Body on earth.

Jesus' Presence in the Spirit

By the "Mystical Body" we mean the Church—all those who have been reborn through Baptism and are living as members of the Body of Christ on earth. In them and through them Jesus continues to speak and act today in the measure that each is docile to the inspirations and promptings of the Holy Spirit. This is the second way Jesus is present in the Mass: through his Spirit speaking in the members of his Body on earth.

This action of the Holy Spirit is not confined to the priest. The Spirit acts in every member of Christ's Body, in each member of the congregation. Each receives gifts of the Spirit to be used for the good of the community. No one comes to the Mass empty-handed; *each has something to contribute* to the overall experience of God acting through his people at Mass.

St. Paul writes to the Ephesians that Jesus ascended into heaven "that he might fill all men with his gifts" (4:10). These gifts are all manifestations of the Spirit acting in Christ's Body on earth today.

And, as Paul says, the Spirit gives the people a great variety of gifts: "To one the Spirit gives wisdom in discourse, to another the power to express knowledge. Through the Spirit one receives faith. . . ," and so on (1 Cor 12:8-9).

Many Catholics are used to the image of the priest doing most of the action at Mass: The priest used to read the Scripture, preach, say all the prayers and even recite alone the parts meant to be sung! Only since Vatican II has the Mass appeared more as the action of a *team*: Now we have lectors, commentators, lay ministers of the Eucharist, etc. Soon, let us hope, it will be evident to all that the Mass is the action of a *whole congregation*.

It was this way in the early Church. Saint Paul had to beg the congregation to moderate their self-expression at Mass: "If any are going to talk in tongues let it be at most two or three, each in turn. . . . Let no more than two or three prophets speak. . . . If another, sitting by, should happen to receive a revelation, the first one should then keep quiet. You can all speak your prophecies, but one by one. . . . God is a God, not of confusion, but of peace" (1 Cor 14:27-33).

If St. Paul could see us now! That teenage boy in Chapter 1 said the church reminded him of a mausoleum. St. Paul was in favor of peace during Mass, but not the peace of the *tomb*! Today it's a lively congregation if you can get people farther back than the first 10 pews to open their mouths and sing!

But in St. Paul's day the action of the Holy Spirit was manifest through what each member of the congregation said and did to contribute to the faith experience of all. In one the gift of wisdom was apparent; in another the gift of knowledge, or of deep faith, or of healing. There were "apostles, prophets, evangelists, pastors and teachers," all of them sharing what they had received from God "in roles of service for the faithful" (Eph 4:11-12).

The point is that these early Christians knew themselves to be members of the Body of Christ, reborn through the gift of new life in grace. They knew the Holy Spirit had been sent into their very beings by the Father and the Son to enrich them with spiritual gifts for the upbuilding of the Body of Christ.

Each and every Christian is gifted by God to help bring the faith and knowledge of every member of the Church to its completeness. This is not just the role of priests and religious. It is the role, the duty and the privilege of every Christian, of every member of the community of believers.

We worry today about a shortage of priests, a "lack of vocations" to the priesthood and to religious life. I am sure there is such a shortage. But it may be God's own providential way of reeducating us to a proper understanding of the Church—and of each one's role within it.

The Church has within itself everything that is needed for the life and growth of the faithful—all the spiritual gifts. But we have to know where to look for them. These gifts are not confined to priests and religious.

The gift of priesthood is one particular vocation and gift. The call to religious life is another. But these are only two among the many, many gifts and "roles of service" required and present in the Church. We should stop thinking in terms of how many priests, brothers and sisters we have, and think instead of discovering and using the *gifts of the Holy Spirit present in the congregation.*

This is the second presence of Christ which we should experience at Mass—and, of course, in the total life of the parish outside of Mass. This is the presence of Christ living, inspiring, speaking in the members of his Body on earth through the gifting presence and power of the Holy Spirit.

Jesus' Presence in the Eucharist

The third presence of Christ in the Mass is his Real Presence in the Eucharist—the reality of his body and blood upon earth. Without this presence his other two forms of presence—through his Word and through the Spirit speaking in the members of his Body—are not complete.

In the Eucharist Jesus himself is made present— really and not just symbolically—under a form that expresses to every man in every age the whole reality of Jesus' historical life upon earth and its meaning: his birth as the peace-child at Bethlehem, his preaching, his healing miracles, his passion and death. Everything he expressed through his word and gesture while on earth are all there, addressed immediately to us.

Scripture is the record of Christ's life, transmitted to us by faithful witnesses through the ages. It is a record through which God speaks with a living voice today. But the Eucharist goes further: It is the *reality* of Christ's life made present to us today. It is Jesus the eternal witness, whose testimony to the Father is presented immediately to our hearts and minds through his Real Presence under the form that symbolically expresses the whole significance of his life: the wheat that falls into the ground and dies to become the food, the life, of the world; the grapes pressed dry of their (juice) blood to become the wine, the joy of the wedding feast.

Through the Scriptures we know what Jesus said; through the Eucharist we know he is saying it to us right now. The Eucharist holds within itself the power of the Body and Blood of Christ.

Just as Scripture alone is not enough, neither is Christ's presence in his Mystical Body. Of course Jesus continues to work, speak and act on earth today through his risen Body on earth—the Church. By the power of his Spirit acting in the members of his Church, he teaches; exhorts; declares sins forgiven; prays; heals; gives alms to the poor; visits the lonely, the sick and the imprisoned; works to reform the structures of political and social life, to bring the spirit of the gospel to the home and the marketplace, to the realities of marriage and business. But his action in every case is limited to some degree by the sinfulness of the members in and through whom he acts.

Jesus truly forgives sins in the sacrament of Penance; but the human impact of his forgiving love is conditioned by the human nature of the minister through whom he acts. Jesus truly expresses his love through each and every person who is a member of his Body; but no person is able to express the love of God for man as Jesus was able to express it through his own human nature, through the reality of his own Body delivered on the cross, his own Blood poured out from his open heart.

All three presences are necessary. In the Scriptures it is Jesus himself who speaks to us. He is present to us in his word. In the Mystical Body we have the risen Jesus truly teaching and bearing witness today, but subject to the limitations and distortions of the sinful human natures of the members through whom he works. In the Eucharist Jesus is present under the appearances of bread and wine, the reality of Jesus—pure and simple. Together these three presences make the Mass a way of "remembering the Lord" that is varied but complete.

The Power of Ritual

The full reality of Christian community is not just a matter of common beliefs and purposes. We are "one Body," one "in the Spirit," one like the grains of wheat which have ceased to be individual grains and have found a new identity as bread. Our unity is on the level of what we *are*; not just on the level of what we *do* together.

That is why the expression of Christian community is not complete unless we pass beyond the Liturgy of the Word into the Liturgy of the Eucharist.

With the Liturgy of the Eucharist we enter into something that goes beyond speaking and listening to God, something more than a prayer service. We engage in a *ritual* in the most complete meaning of the word, a meaning that we have perhaps lost sight of in our modern civilization.

A ritual is a "rite of passage," a symbolic gesture through which a person asks for and accepts a *new identity*. To "speak" in symbolic gestures is more powerful than words; it engages our being more deeply. To speak in symbols is to recognize that one is dealing with mystery: with something—and Someone who acts beyond human powers of comprehension or accomplishment. Ritual is a way of surrendering oneself to forces beyond the human—and is not to be taken lightly; not to be played with. That is why, in the early Church, non-committed Christians (catechumens) were asked to leave when the Liturgy of the Eucharist began.

Ritual is powerful. For example, a ritualistic worship of the devil is much more dangerous and destructive of man's freedom than a mere profession in words of submission to the demonic. The man who talks satanism is blaspheming; but the man who goes through the *ritual* of a satanistic cult is delivering himself up to something he is not able to measure in advance.

All evil is a perversion of the good. Sinful ritual is a perversion of sacred ritual. The Mass is sacred ritual.

In the Mass each member of the congregation is symbolically offering himself to God with the bread and wine. In the Eucharistic Prayer three things happen (which are really all aspects of one and the same reality):

1) All members of the congregation offer themselves with the bread and wine to be transformed into the Body of Christ. All personally accept and reaffirm the act by which we, too, die on the cross in Christ and rise in him to live a new, a transformed life. All offer themselves with Christ and in Christ on the cross and make Christ's act of self-immolation their own.

2) The sacrifice of Jesus on the cross at Calvary is made sacramentally present to the congregation. It is not *repeated*: Jesus died one time for all; his sacrifice can never be repeated. But the one, unique, numerically-same sacrifice of Calvary is made present to us today.

3) The bread and wine are changed into the Body and Blood of Christ.

Finally, in receiving Communion, each participant speaks an "Amen" of faith to the proclamation, "This is the Body of Christ." And each speaks an "Amen" of commitment implied in receiving Jesus' Body and Blood as food: "Amen, I also am the Body of Christ. Amen, I will *live* as the Body of Christ in all I do."

It is easy to see why the Mass meant so much to the Christians of the early Church and why it was such a support to them. They were a persecuted people. They came together in secret before dawn, gathering together out of the darkness—both literal and metaphorical—which surrounded them. They came to gather for a moment in the light of Christ, to draw clarity and strength from his light in order to confront again the darkness of the pagan world in which they lived (a world very much like our own!).

They experienced his light shining from the Scriptures. They saw it reflected on the faces of their fellow believers and discerned its presence anointing the words of others. And then, with the consecration of the bread and wine, Jesus himself was there: the Way, the Truth, and the Life; the true Light which enlightens man's heart; the Light of the world, which shines on in the darkness that cannot overcome it.

In the Eucharist, the "breaking of the bread," they realized anew, like the disciples on the road to Emmaus, that Jesus had not left them alone: "When he had seated himself with them to eat, he took bread, pronounced the blessing, then broke the bread and began to distribute it to them. With that their eyes were opened and they recognized him" (Lk 24:30-31).

The essence of a worshiping Christian community is to be an assembly of believers who "*remember the Lord*," and in so doing *make him present* through their remembrance. In this way Christians support one another in the basic belief upon which all our hopes and lives are founded: "Christ has died; Christ is risen; Christ will come again."

The Secret: Sharing What We Have

When the crowds followed Jesus out into the desert to hear his words, they so lost track of time that it was nearly sundown before they began to realize that they didn't have any shelter or provisions, and the night was coming on. The apostles came and pointed this out to Jesus:

"Dismiss the crowd so that they can go into the villages and farms in the neighborhood and find themselves lodging and food, for this is really an out-of-the-way place" (Lk 9:12).

"Why do you not give them something to eat yourselves?" Jesus answered (9:13).

"Because we don't have anything. Even with a whole year's wages we couldn't buy enough bread to give each person a mouthful!"

So Jesus told them to look around in the crowd and see if anybody had anything to eat.

They went out and came back to report that they had found one small boy who had five loaves of bread—not even wheat bread, but barley—and a couple of dried fish. A real haul!

Jesus told them to have the people sit down. Then, "Jesus then took the loaves of bread, gave thanks, and passed them around to those reclining there; he did the same with the dried fish, as much as they wanted" (Jn 6:11). And then he had his disciples gather up the leftovers: 12 large baskets!

The lesson should not be lost on us. There are in the Christian community sufficient resources for all of our needs. God's Word, Christ's presence, the gifts of the Holy Spirit. These resources are spread out, diffused throughout the community in the form of natural talents and spiritual gifts.

We need not run around to "farms and villages," to fads and movements, looking for the bread that nourishes our souls. It is in our midst: Jesus is here. His Word is here. We are here. We have only to share, and to encourage others to share, the gifts that we have.

Our gifts may not seem like much to us. To the little kid in the Gospels, his five loaves and couple of dried fish must not have appeared very adequate for the needs of 5,000 people. But he gave them, without asking any questions. And the Lord multiplied them.

If each one of us will put at the service of the community, and of the world, the little gift we have—a suggestion, a prayer, an insight, a moment of service, a smile, half a barley loaf, or the tail of a fish—then, even if our combined resources are about as adequate to the world's problems as the five barley loaves and two dried fish to the 5,000, it will be enough. Jesus will take what we are willing to share; he will give thanks, bless it and multiply it.

And there will be baskets left over.

Facing the World Together in Prayer

CHAPTER NINE: *The Salt in the Shakers*

The truth *celebrated* in worship has to become the truth *enacted* in our lives; otherwise our worship is self-deception. If we celebrate the presence of the Lord at worship but do not incarnate that presence at work, in political life, at home and in all our social contacts, we are "remembering the Lord" only to go away and forget immediately what we have remembered.

James puts it this way in his epistle: "A man who listens to God's word but does not put it into practice is like a man who looks into a mirror at the face he was born with: he looks at himself, then goes off and promptly forgets what he looked like" (1:23-24).

A Christian community is a body of people who "remember the Lord" when they turn to face the problems and potentialities of their society: of family, business, social and political life.

In this way the Christian community is not only *supportive* of one another in faith; it is also *creative*. Shared light sheds light. In Christian community members help one another to direct the light of the gospel to the reality of the world around them.

The Challenge: Reforming Society

Probably the greatest challenge of our day is the *Christian reform of society*. This is not the same as a "Christian society"—one in which everyone in the country would be Christian. (When we had a Catholic society of this sort in Europe during the Middle Ages, it is very doubtful how Christian the society itself was. The sins of the "Christian countries" are too numerous to go into here.)

What is the difference between a Christian society and a Christian *reform* of society?

A society can be reformed along Christian lines without all, or even the majority of, citizens ever accepting Christian beliefs. Not everything that is Christian depends on the gospel for its intelligibility or justification. It may have taken the gospel to *call our attention* to some truth or other; but once we have looked and seen, we can say, on the basis of the evidence itself, "This is right and just!"

Many societies have been reshaped (or corrupted, depending on your point of view) along American lines without ever accepting all the principles Americans believe in. Business practices and industrial know-how; long hair, blue jeans, rock music and mini-skirts; universal suffrage and the de-domestication of women: these have profoundly affected the thinking and conduct of millions of people in countries outside of America. These people have taken over many values—good and bad—from American culture. But they have not by that fact "converted" to being American instead of what they were before.

A Christian reform of society frankly offers to the members of society values which Christians believe are better values *in themselves* and which will *prove* to be better values (more productive of healthy, happy life upon earth) if embodied in the structures of society and given a chance.

It can be argued that democracy as we understand it today is such a value. There is no doubt that the founders of American democracy were inspired by Christian principles, tradition and philosophy, even though in many cases their actual, working religion might not have been Christian at all, but the rationalistic deism of the Age of Enlightenment.

There are many other examples one can speculate about: Did the place of women in society evolve under the influence of Christian principles? Did Christianity finally force us to face the issue of racism? Has Christianity made us more conscious of our obligation to help the developing nations? Is Christianity responsible for the state's assumption of responsibility to care for the poor, the sick, the orphaned? Has Christianity had any effect on the concept and conduct of war? On the treatment of prisoners in jail?

Whatever good we might trace to the influence of Christianity in these areas, it is not a good formally adopted by any nation today precisely *because* it is a Christian value. The leaven works in the dough, not to transform the dough itself into leaven, but to make the dough rise. If society becomes healthier and happier through the influence of active Christians, then good has been accomplished.

People in a healthy society will be better prepared to listen to the Good News when and if it is preached to them. But whether it is preached or not, and whether they accept it or not, the Christian reform of society is in itself an effort we believe to be God's will. The world belongs to Jesus the Lord as its creator and redeemer; we, his stewards, must care for it the best we can until he comes again.

We haven't been doing a very satisfactory job.

Christians just don't seem to be reshaping society as successfully as non-Christians are. To leave aside the more complex questions of justice and politics for the moment, consider the effect on American society of two very recent "reforms": the permission for pornography to "go public," and the legalization of abortion. Who brought these about?

When you consider the structures of our society that need reshaping and reforming, one has to wonder what the Christians in America were doing all those years when we were such a church-going nation. Family life is in serious trouble; so are the schools; so is the prison system; so are the nursing homes for the aged; so are the state mental hospitals; so is morale—and morality—in the business world and in politics. Poverty seems more downright destructive in the context of our modern society than ever before; drugs are rampant; sex has gone beyond promiscuity and into publicized perversion; children have no respect for adults; and parents show very little concern about their children. Crime has reached proportions none of us has ever experienced before. It's a lucky family today that can survive for long without some member getting mugged, raped, pregnant before marriage, busted for drugs, picked up for drunkenness, or investigated for tax fraud or illegal contributions to politicians.

We used to read the first chapter of Romans with a wondering shudder at the corruption of pagan Rome. Now it sounds like a description of the United States: "They engaged in the mutual degradation of their bodies. . . . Their women exchanged natural intercourse for unnatural, and the men gave up natural intercourse with women and burned with lust for one another. . . . They are filled with every kind of wickedness: maliciousness, greed, ill will, envy, murder, bickering, deceit, craftiness. They are gossips and slanderers, they hate God, are insolent, haughty, boastful, ingenious in their wrongdoing and rebellious toward their parents. One sees in them men without conscience, without loyalty, without affection, without pity. They know God's just decree that all who do such things deserve death; yet they not only do them but approve them in others" (Rom 1:24-32).

This may not sound like a description of your own circle of friends. But it could be amply documented in every detail as a description of large segments of American society from the top to the bottom rungs of the social ladder. Most of it could be documented from the history of Watergate alone!

Where is the Leaven?

If this is the dough, what has the leaven been doing? Where has the "light of the world"—as Christ described his followers—been shining? Is this the taste that we, the "salt of the earth," are imparting to our society? Or has the salt itself lost its flavor? (See Mt 5:13-16.)

I would suggest two reasons why Christianity is not having its reforming effect on society. The first reason I will present below; the second I will explain in the following chapter. But they both come down to an absence of *lay spirituality*.

I don't mean by this that the fault belongs to the laity rather than to the clergy and religious. I mean that all of us—clergy, religious and laity alike—have neglected, or perhaps been unconscious of, the true nature of the spirituality of the layperson. The priests haven't preached it; the religious haven't taught it; the laity haven't practiced it. Not, at least, until very recently. Now it is beginning, I think, to come into its own.

The spirituality of the layperson is to be the leaven *in* the dough, not outside of it. It is *in* and *through* family life, social life, business life, political life that lay Christians must grow in holiness.

The monk works on holiness in the monastery; the layperson in the market place. A layperson can *visit* a monastery—or a church, a retreat house or Cursillo center—for spiritual rest and recuperation, for inspiration and clarification of a faith vision. But his real growth takes place on the job—at home, in shop or office, when voting or buying or recreating.

(This notion of secular spirituality is drawn from three documents of Vatican II: *The Constitution on the Church*, especially chapters four and five; *The Church in the Modern World*; and *The Apostolate of the Laity*. No one can aspire to a serious spiritual life as a Christian layperson today without reading these documents.)

The first reason why Christianity is having so little effect on society is that *Christians are not trained to put the two together*. In Chapter 6 we spoke of the split between religion and "practical" matters in one's *personal* life. Here we want to look at how this split is found—and perpetuated, even promoted—in the life and interaction of the Christian *community*.

In a Gallup poll on the attitudes of U.S. Catholics conducted for *Newsweek* in 1971, "Nine out of 10 respondents were unable to name a single decision by the National Conference of Catholic Bishops that they considered important to their lives" (*Newsweek*, Oct. 4, 1971). Does this indicate a leadership failure on the part of the bishops? Or a mindset on the part of the laity not to look to religion for any direction about the "real" things of life?

Anyone who reads the publications coming out of the United States Catholic Conference knows that the bishops are saying plenty today that is "important to our lives." Whether we are *hearing* it is another question.

Wherever the blame is to be laid, the overwhelming evidence of the *Newsweek* survey is that American Catholics were brought up within the Christian community to look upon religion as a very personal, private and individualistic matter—as if one's obligations to God and fellow man were fulfilled by simply *not* doing anything bad oneself. "There was little in our experience of private confession which prepared us for making a real examination of our social conscience," says Philip Scharper, 52, a Catholic editor and essayist. "And we have yet to learn to judge our actions in relation to Christ's call for justice, peace and reconciliation of all men."

A priest I know who had the difficult task of integrating a black parish and a white parish into one in southern Louisiana told me one day after it was all (peacefully) over: "You know, we confronted the question of racial attitudes, integration and segregation at every single turn of parish life. You couldn't decide on anything, from the altar boys' picnic to the Mass schedule, without the question of integration coming up. It came up everywhere, except in one place: *It never came up in the confessional—* at least, hardly ever."

The Catholics in that parish were not accustomed to thinking of their *religion—*of their sins and virtues—as having anything to do with their *racism.* Religion concerned *sins—*things like impatience, cussing, sexual faults, stealing and the like. Racial integration was a question of *social structure.* You wouldn't confess "sociology" in the confessional, would you?

Vatican II says you should. The Council strongly condemns those Catholics "who think that religion consists in acts of worship alone and in the discharge of certain moral obligations" which do not include the reform of social structures.

"Let there be no false opposition between professional and social activities on the one part, and religious life on the other. The Christian who neglects his temporal duties neglects his duties toward his neighbor and even God, and jeopardizes his eternal salvation," states the *Pastoral Constitution on the Church in the Modern World* (43).

This means the Christian community should face, and face *together* in faith and in prayer, the question of Christian response to the way our society is going, or failing to go.

At the present time the Catholic community does not seem to have an adequate structure set up to do this. Nor do we really know what it is all about. But we can learn.

An Example of How to Begin

One man we can learn from is John Woolman. Woolman was a Quaker. He lived just before the American Revolution (1720-1772). He was one of the first Christians in this country to seriously confront the issue of slavery. He describes in his diary how the confrontation began. The following quotes are taken from *The Journal of John Woolman*, edited by Janet Whitney (Regnery, 1950).

"Within a year after my coming to Mount Holly, my master having a Negro sold her and told me to write a bill of sale. The thought of writing an instrument of slavery for one of my fellow creatures gave me trouble," Woolman confesses, "and I was distressed in my mind about it." At length, however, Woolman was able to talk himself into writing the bill of sale. After all, "I was hired by the year" and "my master [himself a Quaker] bid me do it."

Yet Woolman's conscience was not clear. "I was depressed in my mind and said before my master and the friend that I believed slavekeeping to be a practise inconsistent with the Christian religion; saying so abated my uneasiness; yet as often as I reflected seriously upon it I thought I should have been clearer if, leaving all consequences, I had craved to be excused from it, as a thing against my conscience; for such it was."

Some time later, when another Quaker asked Woolman "to write an instrument of slavery," he took a firm stand: "After a short prayer I told him I was not easy to write it, for though many people kept slaves in our Society as well as others, and seemed easy in it, I, however, could not see it to be right, and craved to be excused from it."

Had Woolman stopped here, his story would be an inspiring example of a personal break *on the individual level* with the civil religion insofar as it was affecting, and infecting, his own religious community. He would be a marvelous example of a man who was willing to stand alone with his conscience against nonbelievers and fellow believers alike. But Woolman's story doesn't stop here.

He made it his mission in life to bring his faith community, his fellow Quakers, to confront the inconsistency between Christianity and slaveholding. In private conversation he bore witness to his conscience. Sometimes he found a receptive, friendly response; sometimes he encountered hostility.

Woolman took his stand in action as well as in words. He would not write a will—and apparently he was much in demand for this—if the transmission of slaves was included in it. Also, Woolman refused to come even as a guest into the homes of slaveowners, or to accept any gifts from them. He wished to avoid any appearance of compromise or collaboration.

Through all of this, Woolman learned never to let himself speak out of anger or human aggressiveness.

He imposed silence on himself until he was "certain of sufficient inner experience" and able to speak with calmness, sympathy and tenderness.

He was not a wild horse, taking the bit of social reform in his mouth. Rather, as he says in his journal, "I found by experience that to keep pace with the gentle actions of Truth, and never more but as that opens the way, is necessary for the true servants of Christ."

Both in speech and in action Woolman was learning the difference between being guided by the spirit of this world—pride, anger, hatred, the desire to dominate, crush and achieve—and by the spirit of God—a spirit of love, humility, gentleness and concern for all, of obedience and desire to be used by God for God's own purposes, not for one's own.

Woolman was a man able to speak to his faith community because he was a man who spoke constantly with God. And he listened—with a humble, discerning heart to the voice of God speaking to him. He was a prophet.

Because of his docility to God, his efforts were able to bear fruit. As Woolman says "The Lord, who was near me, preserved my mind in calmness under some sharp conflicts, and begat a spirit of sympathy and tenderness in me towards some who were grievously entangled in the spirit of the world."

John Woolman was no more than 21 years old when his confrontation with slavery began. He worked long and perseveringly the rest of his life for the abolition of slavery in the Quaker communion. He suffered for it, and in his suffering turned not to anger and revolution, but deeply inwards to his God.

In 1758 the Quakers voted in their annual meeting to end the purchasing of slaves and to visit those Friends who kept slaves. John Woolman was assigned to the mission of traveling to persuade his coreligionists to free the slaves they owned. He kept at this task for the next 14 years, and like most true prophets, died without seeing the realization of what he worked for. Four years after his death, in 1776, the Quakers of Pennsylvania voted to free all their slaves.

The Key: Listening and Praying Together

So far we have spoken of the prophetic *person* of John Woolman. But why was his religious community able to *listen* to his prophetic message when other Christian communities—the Catholic, for example, as well as other Protestant communities—did not hear the prophets that must have been in their midst?

At the risk of oversimplification, I would like to suggest one very important, and perhaps decisive, cause: the nature of the Quaker prayer meeting.

In terms of procedure (we are not speaking here of underlying beliefs or principles), there is no essential difference between the Quaker prayer meeting and the first part of the Mass. The Liturgy of the Word is essentially nothing but a prayer meeting:

an assembly of believers in which Christ is remembered and made present through his scriptural Word and his Spirit speaking through the members of his Body on earth.

But in terms of practical effects, there is one very crucial difference between the Quaker meeting and the prayer service portion of the Mass: In the Catholic Mass the priest and lectors are conducting the real action during the prayer service, while in the Quaker meeting the members of the congregation are interacting spiritually with one another. In this difference, the Quaker meeting is probably closer to the authentic Liturgy of the Word of the early Mass.

Catholics may react in their hearts to what is read or preached by the ministers at Mass, but never spontaneously out loud. They do not interact with one another. If you want to know what is, or was, going on in a Catholic's heart during Mass, you wait until you get out the front door; then he or she will tell you.

In a Quaker meeting, however, any member can read a passage from Scripture that seems appropriate to the occasion. Any member can speak a prayer out loud, or start a hymn, or share with the assembly something in his mind and heart that he feels the community should reflect on. In this sense, the Quaker meeting is closer to what St. Paul describes as the Liturgy of the Word of the early Church: "When you assemble, one has a psalm, another some instruction to give, still another a revelation to share" (1 Cor 14:26).

Of course there is danger of disorder in such a service. And St. Paul had to correct the early Christians on this score. But there is also the possibility of confronting new challenges as a community interacting in prayer.

If John Woolman had been a Catholic layperson, it is hard to imagine where he could have gotten a prayerful hearing for the things he had to say. Had he preached abolition of slavery from the pulpit as a priest or as a Protestant minister, he would probably have succeeded only in alienating and angering his audience. In a typical Sunday-morning congregation the people "out there" in the pews are at most *listening* to the preacher; they are not *praying along* with him.

To be able to receive challenging, prophetic words a congregation must be prayerfully reflecting in silence on those words. They must also hear others in the congregation speak in response—not their intellectual arguments or their emotions, but the reactions they are discerning as the action of God in their hearts. It is not enough for John the Baptist to preach; the community has to respond through prayer and encouragement of one another; "Let us go see."

I have already written in another place of "contemplative listening."[1] A Christian community, gathered in prayer, listens contemplatively when each

---

1. See chapter nine of my book on religious life: *Cloud by Day, Fire by Night: The Religious Life as Passionate Response to God*, published as part of the *Vita Evangelica* series by the Canadian Religious Conference, 324 Laurier Ave. East; Ottawa, 1976.

member present listens with one ear to the person who is speaking; listens with the other ear to the reactions of his own heart to what is said; and all of this time keeps his eyes fixed on the face of God as his criterion of evaluation.

John Woolman could be a prophet to his faith community because that community was not really responding to Woolman, but to the voice of God in their hearts confirming or negating what Woolman proposed.

For a faith community to do this there has to be a structure of worship that allows it. You can hardly expect 500 people, facing the back of each other's head in an auditorium-style church, with a 30-second pause after the sermon, to respond deeply and contemplatively to something prophetic from the pulpit.

But you can hardly get rid of the churches, or ask 450 of the people to stay home! We're talking about reform, not about revolution. Reforms grow slowly, and they begin small.

What we are doing here is just setting forth the need—a burning need in our times—for Catholic communities to find a way to *let the gospel confront their lives together in prayer*. This can begin in parish councils, in prayer groups, in committee meetings, in the daily prayer of rectories and convents. Husbands and wives can let the gospel confront their lives together as a family in this way. People in business, or in the same social circle, can gather to confront together in prayer their business practices, their social etiquette.

What if Christian women in a town prayed together over the clothes styles they would and would not accept from New York? We are not speaking of a pastor denouncing immodesty from the pulpit by the standards of a monk or a celibate, but of Christian women letting God speak in their hearts—out loud to one another.

What if a parish divided into groups to seriously pray over the corporate attitude and image (let us say "witness") of the parish with regard to ethnic groups, blacks, the poor?

What if parents subjected to examination in the light of the gospel the recreational patterns society provides their children?

A mother whose daughter was just entering Catholic high school complained that the school's "get acquainted" dance for ninth-graders required each girl to have an escort. "This means they have to start one-on-one dating in the eighth or ninth grade," she told me. "I don't like it, not one bit. But what am I going to do? Tell her to stay home? Why can't we get the kids acquainted without pairing them off two-by-two when they're 13?"

What countervailing force can the Christian community provide to the culture? The answer is *not* to band together in pressure groups to boycott stores, picket movie theaters, start parish recreational centers, put on political campaigns. These things might be good at times. But what I am proposing is that Christians sit down together and *let God speak* in their hearts. That they let the gospel confront their lives. That they engage, not in heated, emotional, intellectual discussions, but in prayerful listening together.

It is an axiom that when men shout, God drops his voice to a whisper. We must learn to be silent together and listen to our hearts. In this way we will act, not out of our *convictions* (which are often a disguise for the prejudices inherited from our culture), but out of our *experience of being moved interiorly by God*.

The person moved by God is not a pusher, not a revolutionary, not a would-be messiah using a "cause" to establish a better self-image or to find meaning and fulfillment in life.

The person moved by God acts, not out of a desire to control, but out of a necessity to obey. As John Woolman writes: "I cannot write thy will without breaking my own peace"; "I found myself under a necessity in a friendly way to labour with them on that subject."

Catholics Who Didn't Pray Together

Before we close this chapter, it would be helpful, though humbling, to look at the Catholic side of the scoreboard. We have our story of slavery too. Father John LaFarge, S.J., records it in his autobiography.

In post-colonial days, the Jesuits in southern Maryland had extensive plantation holdings—and slaves. In 1838, 62 years after the Quaker decision, the Jesuits decided it was not proper for them to be slaveowners.

There is no evidence of their having prayed together over the decision. Rather, the provincial at the time prayed in his heart alone, then wrote to the General in Rome. And the General also prayed in his heart alone, then wrote back that they should get rid of the slaves—not by freeing them, but by selling them.

The Jesuits' consciences were probably distracted from the issue by the fact that Father General insisted on "certain humane conditions to be strictly observed" in the sale of the slaves. They apparently focused more on the humane conditions to be observed in the sale than on the inhumane reality of the sale itself. They did not pray *together* before God over the decision that was made.

When Father LaFarge arrived on the scene 75 years after the event, it was still alive in the memories of the descendants of those Negroes involved in the sale. Even the names of the characters, good and bad, were fresh in the mind of the old black lady who told him this story related in *The Manner Is Ordinary* (Harcourt, Brace and Co., 1954):

"Father Carberry was terribly unhappy about it. He prayed and he prayed and he pleaded with the Fathers and begged that such a dreadful thing might not happen. He told the folks that he was praying, and asked them to pray with him." But the Jesuits "outvoted him," she recalled.

"When the time came for the wicked men to take the Negroes away, Father Carberry warned some of them about it and so a few of them escaped," she continued. "People wept and cried when the ship came that took them away. Once they were gone the people who had stayed came out of the woods and Father Carberry welcomed them; he was so happy that at least some had escaped.

"He was a good and holy man. Why were there not more like Father Carberry?" she asked.

The question really isn't, "Why were there not more like Father Carberry?" There probably were. Probably most of the men involved in this transaction—on the wrong side—were as holy as he was. (At least nobody is going to catch us Catholics admitting that the membership, by and large, of the Society of Jesus in Maryland in 1832 was not as holy and open to the Word of God as the membership of the Society of Friends in Philadelphia in 1776! Our side must have had as many "good guys" as their side!

The real question is, "Why wasn't Father Carberry able to be a prophet to the Society of Jesus in the way that John Woolman was to the Society of Friends?"

I think the answer to that question can be found in the way they prayed—or didn't pray—together. And that raises the question of how *we* pray—or don't pray—together.

The Key to Lay Spirituality

CHAPTER TEN: *Monk or Martyr: the Christian Choice*

This is not a book on Christian social action. It is a book about encountering Christ. But encounter with Christ is not real unless the person I have met as Jesus Christ is radically influencing my life—transforming my life at its roots. And Christ is not transforming my life if I am not affecting the people around me in a Christian way. Fire gives off heat, lamps give off light. If a stove isn't heating, the fire has gone out. And if a lamp is under a bushel you can be sure its flame has been extinguished or will be extinguished very soon.

The same is true of a Christian community—a Christian family, organization, parish. If the community is not confronting and responding to the problems of its own environment, its own milieu, it is not a community that has a live relationship with Christ. Where two or three are gathered together in his name, he is in the midst of them; and Christ does not stand around idle.

We have said that the essential elements of real encounter with Christ are *prayer*, *conversion* and *community*. In prayer we must reflect on the Word of God until we come to decisions that change our lives. Through conversion we must reorient our lives toward the Kingdom of God from the roots up. In the midst of community we must support one another in faith and help each other to leaven the dough we live in—that is, to witness to Christ in prophetic contradiction of the spirit of this world.

Why do we fail so often to do this?

At the heart of our failure to really experience Christ in our hearts and to express his reality in our lives is our failure to pray. We do not pray as we should, either individually or together. As we saw in the last chapter, we do not pray in a way that brings our lives and the life of our society into confrontation with the gospel.

Admittedly we haven't been trained to do this. But that excuse no longer exists. Readers who have come this far should know by now what they have to do to encounter the reality of Christ in a way that brings them face to face with the reality of their lives.

But there is another reason for our failure to leaven the society in which we live: We have lost the fundamental concept of lay spirituality.

The Gospels Are Addressed to Lay People

Most of us were brought up with the idea that lay people were second-rate Christians. Those who "wanted to be perfect" became priests or religious. Lay people followed the "way of the commandments": They did what Jesus said you *had* to do. Religious followed the "way of the counsels" (the evangelical counsels of poverty, chastity and obedience): They did what Jesus said it was *better* to do.

The advice Jesus gave to the rich young man, to "sell all you have and give to the poor" and then "come and follow me" (Lk 18:22) was interpreted and preached again and again as if Jesus were calling the young man to be a priest or a religious. In fact, Jesus was calling him to be a Christian and nothing else: nothing more, nothing less.

There is no text in Scripture meant to describe the life-style of priests or religious as such because, at the time the Scriptures were written, priests lived just like everyone else and religious life did not yet exist as a separate life-style in the Church. Everything in the Gospels is meant to teach us what Christianity itself is all about: what is required of *every* person who would be a follower of Jesus Christ; what is promised to *each* one of us.

This can raise a lot of questions in our minds, conditioned as we are to make a distinction between those who "would be perfect" and those who "just want to make it to heaven." We still think of the "state of grace" as a ticket to hold onto, something to get us through the General Admission section of the pearly gates.

Priests, sisters and brothers; monks and nuns—they are the ones who "sold all" on this earth and will have a front-row seat when the curtain falls on this life and rises on the next. The poor lay people, who didn't have the courage to give up "home, brothers or sisters, father or mother, wife or children or property" for Jesus' sake, will "make it" to heaven, but they will be sitting in the back rows thinking of the "hundredfold" that could have been theirs (cf. Mt 19:29).

How did this caricature arise?

Basically it came about through a lot of historical circumstances and developments. But instead of trying to follow the thread backwards through history, unraveling all its knots, let's simply start at the beginning and see what happened.

Martyrdom: the Earliest Spirituality

Let's start with two facts: First, everything in the Gospels was understood in the beginning to apply to all Christians without distinction of categories. Second, all Christians did not in fact sell everything they owned and give it to the poor. Nor did they all "make themselves eunuchs" or renounce sex through a vow of celibacy for the sake of the Kingdom of God (cf. Mt 19:12). Yet they all knew they were called to "be perfect," and they held up the perfection of the Gospels as their ideal.

What, then, was the life-style that the early Church presented to its members as the model of Christian perfection? In one word, it was *martyrdom*.

It may sound strange to call martyrdom a life-style. We associate martyrdom with "dying for the faith," and dying is not something that can become a regular part of one's daily schedule. But if we look at the real meaning of the word *martyr*, we can understand how martyrdom can become a style of life.

The meaning of martyrdom is *witnessing*—but not just any kind of witnessing. The martyrs bore witness with their lives. They professed their faith in blood, not only in words. They proclaimed Jesus Christ with the *word-made-flesh* of their own bodies offered to torture and death. The "stuff" of their witnessing, what made their witness credible, was what they were willing to let go rather than abandon the new "way" of Jesus Christ.

It wasn't the *fact* of renunciation that made the witness of martyrdom real—the actual renouncing of life, liberty or property through execution, imprisonment or fines. Rather, it was the fact that renunciation *might* be called for. Thus a *risk* was knowingly incurred and freely accepted, a risk one lived with all day and every day. This risk was itself the reality of the martyrs' witness to Christ.

To live with the risk of losing everything one cherished was no easier for the early Christians than to just renounce everything from the start by actually giving it up. Compared with the decision to incur this risk by becoming a Christian, and to intensify it by living daily in constant, uncompromising fidelity to the principles of the gospel, the actual moment of arrest or execution must have been something of an anticlimax. Fear is harder to live with than finality. To live day after day without knowing whether tomorrow will bring a knock on the door that means impoverishment, prison or death: this is in many ways harder to bear than the sentence of death itself.

When we define martyrdom as bearing witness to Christ by an uncompromising faithfulness to the teachings and values of Jesus Christ that imperils life, liberty or the normal pursuit of happiness in this world, then martyrdom can indeed be a way of life. And this was the spirituality of the early Church.

This way of life was held up as a model to the first Christians. "To be perfect" was to live in this world without being attached to it—to have one's treasure, and one's heart, in heaven. This did not require actually giving up possessions, wife or children, or the means of earning one's livelihood on this earth.

The first way of holiness held up to Christians was to live—as Vatican II put it many centuries later—in the "ordinary circumstances of family and social life—to live in the world, that is, in each and all of the secular professions and occupations" (*Constitution on the Church*, 31). And it was from these "ordinary circumstances" of family life, business life, social life and political life, that the very web of Christian existence—and of spiritual life—was to be woven.

But Christians were to live in this world without compromising with the values of this world. They were not to let anything in this world—or the fear of its loss—keep them from "seeking first the Kingdom of God and its holiness." To be a Christian was to have already radically relocated one's hopes in heaven.

St. Paul puts it this way: "I tell you, brothers, the time is short. From now on those with wives should live as though they had none; those who weep should live as though they were not weeping, and those who rejoice as though they were not rejoicing; buyers should conduct themselves as though they owned nothing, and those who make use of the world as though they were not using it, for the world as we know it is passing away" (1 Cor 7:29-31).

In other words, enjoy what God gives you, but hold it loosely.

The spirit of Christian martyrdom—as a way of life—is to live for Christ alone; to live the gospel without compromise, and to be unconcerned about the consequences. This spirit of martyrdom is the freedom of the children of God. It's a spirit of radical freedom with regard to every threat or value on this earth.

Christ has risen. Christ has triumphed over every menace to man's existence, over sin and death. Christ has won for us the Kingdom of God. Man is free to live in uncompromising witness to Christ alone and not fear the coming or the going of any value, person, event or thing. The "pearl of great price" is ours; other pearls are as precious as they ever were, but henceforth inconsequential.

The first model of Christian holiness, therefore, was not to actually *give up* the world—to renounce marriage, give one's property away to the poor, drop out of the affairs of this world—but to *let go* of the world—to stop clinging.

Christian martyrs were people who lived the gospel without counting the cost. They held onto the truth and values of Christ with all their strength; the rest they held very loosely. Anything that men, or death, could take away they didn't worry about. In this way their whole life became a constant act of witness to the gospel, because every choice of their life was ruled by the truth and values found in Jesus Christ.

They put their money where their mouth was, because they didn't care whether they held onto it or lost it. Their real treasure was safely hidden in a field that they had already "sold everything" to gain title to.

The Rise of Monasticism

During the time of persecutions, just to be a Christian was to be constituted in a state of martyrdom. One risked everything just by existing as a member of this new "way."

But then the persecutions ceased; the Emperor Constantine was converted. This put the "boss" on our side. To be a Christian was now the "in" thing; to be Christian was to belong to the Establishment.

And this is where the confusion began.

When the Establishment accepted Christianity, we thought that Christianity had absorbed the Establishment. If the government was Christian, then it seemed logical that Christians should be *for* the government.

The emperor said that Christians were no longer a problem to the state; they were a part of the state. So Christians accepted their new status and stopped being a problem. They also stopped bearing witness—prophetic witness, at least—to the society they lived in. As they saw it, you couldn't be a part of the Establishment and a problem—or a prophet—to it at the same time.

Society now called itself "Christian." This tricked Christians into believing that their culture and their religion were really one. After all, the state (which was the expression of their culture) and the Church (which was the expression of their religion) were united. How could it be that religion and culture were not identified? All the "right kind of people" were Christians; therefore, to do what the right kind of people did must be the Christian thing to do.

As a result, Christians began to believe that to call the accepted policies, attitudes or values of their "Christian" society into question was to be, not a Christian witness, but a religious fanatic; not a

martyr, but a heretic. The Christian thing was not
to stand out, or to stand against, but to *fit in*.
Society was "Christian." Hence, to be an accepted
member of society was to be a "good Christian."

This was civil religion pure and simple. When religion and culture are identified, it is not the culture
that has been converted, but Christianity which has
lost its identity. Once a culture begins to think of
itself as "Christian," the Good News is no longer
listened to as news.

What happened next was the discovery of a new
spirituality. In place of the old spirituality of
martyrdom, a new spirituality arose: the spirituality of the monks in the desert.

The first generation of Christians had borne witness
in the City of Man: They lived by the gospel in the
marketplace, and they died for the gospel in the
amphitheatre. Like Jesus they "set their face
toward Jerusalem"; they went *to* the city to be
crucified there.

But the next generation was tricked into believing
that the City of Man and the City of God were one
and the same. They lived in the city and were not
crucified. They were comfortable there. Pretty
soon there was no persecution and no prophecy;
no warfare and no witness.

The inspiring challenge of risking all in witness to
Christ seemed to be a thing of the past. Martyrdom
was no more. And witness was no more. There was
no one to bear witness to. Christianity had been

absorbed into the culture. The dough had absorbed the leaven, but had not risen very much. The water had been mingled with the wine, but in such proportions that it was the wine which lost its taste. Everything was flat and mediocre. And the Christian heart was dissatisfied.

What had happened to the great ideal of "selling all" out of love for Jesus Christ? Where had the dramatic experience of believing in Christ disappeared to?

And so there was a reaction. The monks of the desert were born. If the city had lost its challenge for Christianity, Christians would seek out a new challenge in the desert.

The spirituality of risk, which was martyrdom, was succeeded by the spirituality of renunciation, which was *monasticism*.

At their core the two spiritualities are the same. In both cases the Christian takes a stance toward this world which can only be explained by faith in the gospel of Jesus Christ. The martyr lives in the world risking daily the loss of everything he has. The monk "leaves" the world by giving up everything he has.

In both spiritualities there is a radical renunciation of this world and of all it promises in favor of the Kingdom of God and the promise of Jesus Christ. But the monk expresses this deep, interior "dying to the world" by *actually renouncing* property, marriage and life in the City of Man. The martyr, on the other hand, expresses this "dying to the world" by remaining in the world—by putting down roots in this world by acquiring property, marrying a wife, raising children, and taking part in the City of Man. Yet, at the same time, he lives in such a way that he daily *risks* the loss of everything he has.

Both the monk who refuses to put down roots in this world and the martyr who is ready at any moment to be uprooted are expressing the same radical recentering of their hearts and lives in the truth of the gospel and the promise of the Kingdom of God.

The Christian Mistake

Where Christians made their mistake—and it is a mistake we are only just beginning to notice—was in assuming that the spirituality of martyrdom was *replaced* by the spirituality of monasticism instead of just being supplemented by it. Martyrdom and monasticism are not *successive* spiritualities in the Church but *alternate* spiritualities. One did not replace the other, as if the only way to be a perfect Christian in the beginning was to be a martyr, and the only way now is to be a monk.

The choice of monk or martyr is the choice every Christian faces today. We can choose—or be called to—the spirituality of risk or to that of renunciation. We can stay in the world and bear witness in the City of Man, or we can leave the world and bear witness from the desert.

The spirituality of renunciation—what I have called "leaving the world" for the desert or the monastery—does not mean that one actually, in a geographical sense, moves out of town into the wilderness, or into a monastery. Some do, of course, and these are the ones to whom we give the name "monk" today. (Or we call them "contemplatives" or "cloistered.")

What constitutes "leaving the world" as I mean it is the act of *taking one's stakes* out of the world by the actual renunciation of property, of marriage and children, and of a life lived in the "ordinary circumstances of family and social life. . .in secular professions and occupations" (*Constitution on the Church*, 31). Those who do this are called "religious"—that is, Christians who have taken vows of poverty, celibate chastity and obedience—no matter where they live or how much work they do in the City of Man. By renouncing these fundamental relationships through which man's existence is rooted in this world, they have "left" the world in a real, if not a physical or geographical, sense.

The "world" religious leave is not the world as *bad* (the world as sinful or "worldly") but that world which is precisely the milieu of the lay Christian's sanctification. Religious *disengage* themselves from the relationships of ownership, marriage and secular involvements. But these relationships from which the religious disengage themselves are precisely the relationships "*from which the very web of the lay Christian's existence is woven*" (*Constitution on the Church*, 31; emphasis added).

Life-Style is the Key

The religious—even the sister who may spend 12
to 14 hours a day picking up the dying off the
crowded city streets of Calcutta with Mother
Teresa—is bearing witness out of a monk's life-style.
The difference between a religious and a layperson
is not in the work they do, but in the style of life
each lives. A lay man or woman could do the same
work as Mother Teresa's sisters without becoming a
religious brother, priest or sister.

Our problem today is that we have lost sight of
what constitutes the special, sanctifying characteristic of the *lay* Christian's life-style. We are not
even very aware that lay Christians *have* a life-style
specifically and properly their own. But they do,
and this life-style is the source of what is specific
and proper to lay spirituality.

The lay Christian's life-style is *secularity*; and his
spirituality is *martyrdom*.

"Secularity" means laypersons are called to live in
this world *as a part of it*. They form relationships
with the world through ownership, marriage and
business. They invest in this world, put down roots
in the world and show faith that the world is not
hopelessly bad or irredeemable.

Their real treasure is in heaven, it is true. But they
keep their stakes in this world in a real, if not ultimate, sense. They invest labor and savings in buying a house and in paying for it. They invest their
physical being in children and in raising them to
live in this risky, good-and-bad world. They engage

in business and in politics with a positive spirit, refusing to despair of the world's possibilities.

Theirs is a spirituality of hope in the power of grace, not just to redeem us "out" of this world, to take us beyond it, but also to redeem us *in* the world right now, to redeem the world itself through our graced efforts and gift of self. Lay spirituality believes that the Kingdom of God is for here and now, and that we should work to establish it in all the concrete structures, policies, customs, manners and morals of our everyday world. And the lay person *expresses* this hope by accepting to "spend his days in the midst of the world and of secular transactions," where "he is called by God to burn with the spirit of Christ and to exercise his apostolate in the world as a kind of leaven" (*Decree on the Apostolate of the Laity*, 2).

This is Christian secularity. And the spirituality proper to it is a spirituality of martyrdom. The secular Christian does not bear witness in word only, but "in deed and in truth" (1 Jn 3:18) through the *risk* that necessarily accompanies any truly Christian life lived in "the midst of the world and of secular transactions." What is this risk?

The "Risk" of the Lay Life-Style

We used to think that "saving one's soul" was easier for the religious than for the layperson because the layperson lives in the midst of so many temptations, so many occasions of sin. The truth of the matter, however, is that temptation is the reality of Christian existence *everywhere*. When Christ went out to the desert, he was tempted. When he went into the city, he was crucified. There is no Christian life without struggle. To follow Christ means to take up one's cross, whether we find it in the city or in the desert.

The "world"—in a *good* sense, the world that is the milieu of the lay Christian's sanctification—never has been and never will be a place where Christianity can be completely "at home." No matter how "good" a society or culture, it will never be an environment or milieu that is completely receptive to Christian values and attitudes.

Christians do not consider the world to be "corrupt." But neither do Christians expect the world to be a completely receptive or even "safe" place for the gospel. This is because the "world"—even the "good" world as it actually exists—has two characteristics:

First, the force of *sin* is always at work in the world determining the direction of many of the most powerful elements of human society in professional, social and political life, and even on the level of the family. Because sin is at work in these areas—in every area of human existence—there will always be some threat to the person who tries to live in this world according to Christian principles.

Second, the simple *inertia* of the world, though not positively hostile to Christianity, resists any efforts to lift patterns of thought or behavior into a higher orbit of human activity. Anyone who rocks the boat is likely to stir up some resentment. A person may be praised as a hero later, but at the moment of initiative he risks being stoned.

This means that Christian secularity is, by definition, a state of risk. To live *in* the world—engaged in all the world's activities, a part of all that is going on in the world—and to set one's own course by that light of Christ which comes from *beyond* this world and leads beyond this world: this, by the very nature of things, is to invite trouble. For one thing, it puts one on a collision course with some very powerful forces active in human society. For another thing, it leaves one without the support of those elements in our culture which, though good, are not specifically and primarily directed toward the Kingdom of God and which do not understand why anyone should want to be so "different."

The Christian martyr must resist simultaneously the attacks of enemies and the entreaties of friends. His two great adversaries are the devil and the common man. And to make things even worse, there is a little bit of both in each and every one of us!

I believe we lost the concept of lay spirituality when we assumed—too simplistically—that the age of martyrdom was over. Martyrdom is not something that belongs only to periods of persecution; it belongs to the state of Christian secularity as such. The "age" of martyrdom will be with us as long as the "age" of this world is with us. And there will be, or should be, as many Christian "martyrs"—as we use the word here—as there are Christians living in this world.

Martyrdom was not replaced by monasticism. Monasticism was simply added as a second option. But the spirituality of the vast majority of Christians remains the spirituality of witness *in this world*, in the *saeculum*. This means secular or "lay" spirituality. And this is a spirituality of martyrdom.

To recapture or renew lay spirituality we have to accept a conversion, a change of mind about our whole relationship to this world as Christian laypersons. We have to see ourselves as called, above all and primarily, *to bear witness in the world at our risk*. We have to understand, and accept, and rejoice in the promise and possibilities of the fact that in *every* situation in life we risk paying the price of Christian witness.

There is nothing this world offers that Christians can take for granted, as if faith in Jesus Christ did not automatically place it in jeopardy. By the very fact that we are Christians we risk the loss of everything we could hope for in this world. If we truly "seek first the Kingdom of God and its justice" and live by the truth and values of Jesus Christ in all their depth and fullness, it is not a persecuting government which will declare us outlaws. Society itself will "outlaw" us in much more subtle ways; or at least we run the *risk* of this.

Christians have to accept this risk as the very core of their spirituality, of their relationship to Christ. If we do not, then all of our decisions—more unconsciously than consciously—will be dominated by fear and the pressure to conform to the standards and practices of this world.

Unless we have really "sold" everything we have on the level of our heart and once and for all accepted in advance the loss of all things for the sake of Jesus Christ, we will not have the *courage* to stand against society or the interior *freedom* of mind and spirit to make right judgments about the issues presented to our choice in this world.

A Matter of Mindset

We are talking here about a basic frame of mind, a "mindset." We have to "psyche ourselves up" in order to approach this world, and the choices we have to make in it, from the right perspective.

We grew up believing that *it is possible to be a faithful Christian and lead a "normal" life in this world.* In one sense that attitude is correct, but in another sense, it leads us into all sorts of practical errors in judgment.

If we mean that Christians do not *condemn* this world or *separate* themselves from it, this attitude is perfectly correct. Christians are not against any natural institution in this world, be it marriage, family or social life, business or professional life or politics. We are not against drinking, dancing, dating, buying, selling, voting, learning or going to the movies. In other words, Christians very definitely accept all the normal elements that make up human existence. In this sense Christians do live a "normal" life in this world. As Hilaire Belloc wrote:

> Wherever the Catholic sun doth shine
> There's always laughter and good, red wine.

At least, I've always found it so—
Benedicamus Domino!

Furthermore, Christians accept the complexity of moral choices in this world. We do not think all issues are black and white. We know that politicians have to compromise. (St. Thomas Aquinas defines politics as "the science of the possible": You aim at what you *can* do; not at what, ideally, you would *like* to do.)

We know that one doesn't abstain from drinking or movies entirely because drink can be abused and movies can be dangerous. We don't refuse to do business with everybody who doesn't operate by the highest standards of Christian morality.

If we did not accept the complexity of moral choices in society, we would have to withdraw into ghettoes. We definitely do not believe that Christians should "drop out" of political life, social life, business life or professional activities. We should mix and participate in the life of our society. In this sense too, then, Christians accept a "normal" life in this world.

What I think we have to change in our attitude is not the fact that we *accept* a normal life in this world, but that we *expect* to be able to live one.

I think as Christians, somewhere deep in our hearts, we must give up the expectation that we will be able to "make it" in this world. What we should really expect—and deeply accept, even embrace— is that we will be crucified in this world for the stand we take on the gospel. And we must expect this in every area: in family life, social life, business and professional life, in civic or political life.

Once we expect this, of course, we will do everything possible to keep it from coming about. Having set our course first to "seek the Kingdom of God and its justice" whatever the consequences, we will then use every means God offers us to avoid being ostracized, persecuted, fired, imprisoned, or just shoved off into a corner and forgotten.

As a general rule Christians do not seek the physical reality of martyrdom. What we seek is the Kingdom of God. Actual martyrdom is avoided as long as is possible without compromising the gospel. And to some this can be a scandal.

St. Thomas More had to explain to his rashly-inclined son-in-law William Roper why he used every legal maneuver his "winding wits could find" to avoid coming into headlong confrontation with King Henry VIII. Martyrdom has a certain splendor about it, but as More explains to Roper in *A Man for All Seasons*, by Robert Bolt (Vintage Books, 1962):

"God made the *angels* to show him splendor. . . . But Man he made to serve him wittily in the tangle of his mind! If he suffers us to fall into such a case that there is no escaping, then we may stand to our tackle as best we can, and yes, Will, then we may clamor like champions. . .if we have the spittle for it. . . . But it's God's part, not our own, to bring ourselves to that extremity! Our natural business lies in escaping—so let's get home and study this Bill."

More used all of his wits and training to avoid any word or act that would be an expression of treason against the king. But he would not take the oath that made Henry VIII head of the Church in England. He gave no reason for his refusal—the reason could have been interpreted as treason. He just refused to take the oath. In this he showed the "cleverness of the serpent."

But when More was arrested anyway—and eventually sentenced to death—he showed the "simplicity of the dove." It was, after all, a very simple choice he had to make in the end: refuse the oath or deny the faith. To his daughter Margaret he explained why he would not just speak the words of the oath with his lips, while holding back the intention of his heart:

> Margaret: In any State that was half good, you would be raised up high, not here, for what you've done already. It's not your fault the State's three-quarters bad. Then if you elect to suffer for it, you elect yourself a hero.
>
> More: That's very neat. But look now. . . . If we lived in a State where virtue was profitable, common sense would make us good, and greed would make us saintly. And we'd live like animals or angels in the happy land that *needs* no heroes. But since in fact we see that avarice, anger, envy, pride, sloth, lust

> and stupidity commonly profit far
> beyond humility, chastity, fortitude,
> justice and thought, and have to
> choose, to be human at all. . . , why
> then perhaps we *must* stand fast a
> little—even at the risk of being heroes.

The Christian martyr has to be a person who loves this world. Who wants and tries to live a beautiful, happy family life. Who enjoys people and cherishes their friendship. Who can be enthusiastic about his or her work, and see its human as well as its divine possibilities.

Thomas More was all of this: a humanist, scholar, lawyer and accomplished politician; a husband and father; a writer of poetry and humor, of philosophy and plays. Bernard Basset's *Born for Friendship* is one account of his life; Robert Bolt's *A Man for All Seasons*, cited above, is another. His biographers catch the spirit of the man: He loved life, and he did the best he could to hold onto it.

Christians who bear witness in the world should have great hope and place great trust in God. After all, we have heard Jesus say that if we stop worrying over what we are to eat and drink and what we will have to wear, and seek first the Kingdom of God, "all these things will be given you besides" (Mt 6:33).

Hope and trust are good. The important thing is that we should not *expect* to make it in this world without persecution, or without incurring risk. Because if we do, it is almost inevitable, I think, that our determination of what is Christian will be ruled by our evaluation of what seems compatible with keeping our job, friends, social position, possessions, etc. Then, if it seems obvious to us that a particular stand on the gospel will make it impossible for us to earn a "normal" living, or have a "normal" social life, or do the "normal" things that everybody else does in this particular culture or milieu, we will conclude we are interpreting the gospel wrong; in short, that we are becoming fanatics.

To Give Flesh to His Word

I hope it is clear from what has been said so far that I am not proposing some simple, moral fundamentalism. I know Christians have to weigh very carefully the good and bad consequences, as well as the theoretical pro's and con's, of every moral choice we make. I don't think a person should give up the presidency of the United States rather than shake hands with a communist! I am also very much aware that a delicately balanced Christian choice will often appear to narrower minds as a compromise. But I think in *our* day the great danger is that we have accepted so completely, so uncritically, the assumption that a Christian should be able to live and mix in society "just like anybody else" that we let society, and not the gospel, determine our very judgment of the right and Christian thing to do.

I have already cited some examples of this in Chapter 1 and Chapter 6. In addition, a poll conducted by priest-sociologist Andrew Greeley reveals that in the decade since 1963 the number of Catholics approving of sexual relations between engaged couples has risen from 12 per cent to 43 per cent; those approving of divorce have increased from 52 per cent to 73 per cent; and although there are no figures from 1963 for comparison, 70 per cent of those polled in 1974 think legal abortions should be available for married women who do not want more children.

And these are not even the most complex issues Catholics are asked to judge!

To me this says that very many Catholics really do start from the assumption that a Christian should be able to live in this world just about like everybody else. To the extent that something becomes an accepted practice or attitude in our culture, these Catholics believe it should be a part of the religion too.

Let's take an example a little closer to everyday life. I was once asked to give a talk on sexual morality to girls in the seventh and eighth grades. The talk was good, I think, but it didn't go over. And I finally realized why.

The girls enjoyed the talk. They probably even understood it. They didn't really object to its argumentation. But it just didn't affect them. I was talking about sex—what it is, what principles should govern one's sexual expression—while the girls were concerned about a whole different question.

It was not sex that interested them, or attracted them; it was *belonging* to their peer group. They were beginning to date. Dating was a large part of what it meant to "belong" in that particular social milieu. They knew already that what I was saying about sex and what was standard practice in their social circle were simply not compatible with one another.

As they heard it, to accept what I was saying meant they had to "drop out" of the dating scene. Not to drop out voluntarily, of course, but to "be dropped out." And since the idea of not dating like every-body else *was not even conceivable* to them as a serious choice, they just never "heard" anything I said about the Christian meaning of sex.

The real point isn't whether or not a person who is faithful to Christian ideals in sex will actually be left out of the dating scene. The real point is that these girls—like the rest of us in other areas of life— *took for granted* that if some attitude or ideal would keep them from leading a "normal" life in their own social milieu—"normal" according to the values of their age-group or culture—that atti-tude or ideal *could not be* the correct one.

If they had been leaning in the other direction— which I am calling the attitude of Christian martyr-dom—they would have been looking to Christianity for an ideal of sex so "different" from that of our culture, that the surprising thing would be if they *could* "fit in" to the dating scene as we know it. They would not have judged what was *Christian* by what was *compatible* with their society, but they would have looked to Christ first for an ideal to which they could bear *witness* in society.

And since you can't bear witness on a date unless you have a date, they would have found ways to date and be Christian at the same time. Provided they didn't make dating a *condition* for accepting the Christian ideal, I think Jesus would have arranged for them to have both.

If lay people will accept as their own special spirituality the task of bearing witness *within* society, and if they will embrace from the heart the *risk* that this entails, I think a whole new era will open up in the history of Christianity. The main work of the Church will be borne again, as it should be, by the great majority of Christians, the lay people, instead of being left to the priests and religious.

After all, the "work" of the Church really comes down to only one thing: Christian witness. It is the witness we give to Christ that is the real apostolic value of anything else we do. To reveal Christ's love, his truth; to let his word take flesh in us—that is what it means to be a Christian, a member of the Body of Christ on earth.

How to Walk Alone Together

CHAPTER ELEVEN: *Martyrdom as a Milieu*

Has the spirituality of martyrdom been wholely absent from Catholic consciousness over the centuries? And if it was lacking, who was responsible?

The answers to these questions bring up some important, and very interesting insights into the individual believer's relationship to the broader Christian community.

Most of us grew up very much aware that there were certain things our society considered "normal" that we, as Catholics, could not accept or go along with. In grade school the sisters taught us to take a stand against bad language and dirty jokes. Even then I knew that if I married it would have to be forever; that I could not divorce and marry someone else.

In high school I was actually surprised to learn that some of the boys I knew, my own age though not of my religion, took for granted masturbation and certain sexual intimacies short of intercourse on a date. I knew I had to be "different" in the area of sex.

I also knew we Catholics had to go to Mass *every* Sunday, and was somewhat envious of the Protestants who seemed to have an easier deal. And, of course, in those days Fridays were the test and proclamation of your faith: If you were a Catholic you *didn't* eat meat. We were psyched up from grade school on to die rather than give in over the issue of a hamburger. Finally, as I grew older, I realized that Catholics took a different stand from everyone else on the question of birth control.

And that's all, offhand, that I can remember. To be a Catholic meant to take a stand against the culture on the issues of divorce, sexual morality and birth control. And this was a private stand. It did not involve any public confrontation of society at all. In the public arena, the closest we came to being "martyrs" was refusing to eat meat when it was served on Friday at someone else's house or at a public gathering. And for that challenge, in the Baptist environment in which I grew up, we kept our combat readiness at a peak.

It is easy to lampoon. And before we speak too critically of the religion of those days, we should remember that most of the training we received was given to us in grade school and high school. An uncompromising stand on sexual morality doesn't sound very impressive matched up against the big issues like racial discrimination, social justice, international politics, ecology, pacifism and consumerism. But to take a stand, even a private stand, on sexual issues when you are an adolescent requires—and, I think, develops—a great deal of inner strength and personal, moral courage. It is also one of the most *real* expressions and experiences of faith to be looked for in the life of teens.

Faith is only affirmed in choices that express themselves in *action* in the concrete reality of our actual life situation. For high school students to think they are "real" Christians because they take the right stand—in thoughts and in words—on faraway issues like pacifism, international justice and even racial discrimination *somewhere else* is pure illusion.

We sometimes forget that as grade school and high school kids we didn't have any real *choices* to make in those days in the areas of international politics or social justice. Most of the big, important issues named above were not even part of the ordinary American's vocabulary during this period of the Church.

But sex was very much a part of our vocabulary, and of our moral confrontation. Its challenge was always before us, and in the face of that challenge you either went up or down. To the everlasting credit of our teachers, they at least taught us to confront what was *real* in our lives at that time. Hamburgers on Friday, dirty words in the school-yard and physical passion on a date were very, very real. And according to how we responded to these challenges, Jesus Christ became real in our lives.

In an embryonic state, the spirituality of martyrdom was there. We knew we had to die for Christ rather than deny our faith. And it did come through to us that martyrdom was a real prospect. No one who listened to the Gospels read at Mass could have missed the point that persecution and the cross are presented as a *normal*—and a significant—portion of the Christian expectation.

Matthew's Gospel tells us: "What I am doing is sending you out like sheep among wolves. . . . They will hale you into court, they will flog you in their synagogues. You will be brought to trial before rulers and kings, to give witness. . ." (Mt 10:16-18).

And Mark's says: "If a man wishes to come after me, he must deny his very self, take up his cross, and follow in my steps. Whoever would preserve his life will lose it, but whoever loses his life for my sake and the gospel's will preserve it" (Mk 8:34-35).

We knew that, in some vague way, martyrdom had to be part of our lives; the cross was for everybody. But how?

I personally could not think of martyrdom except in terms of something extraordinary. Perhaps the communists would take over the government and make it a crime to believe. Or someone might, under hard-to-imagine circumstances, try to force me into sin. Aside from that, the only other way I could think of the cross coming into my life was

through some painful, physical illness. So I prayed
for the strength to hold out under torture and to
"offer up" sickness should these be my lot, and
went about living as usual, waiting for martyrdom
to come to me.

It's not that we didn't know we ought to be
martyrs; we just didn't know how to go about it.
We didn't realize that the martyrdom proposed in
the Gospels was something you wouldn't have to
wait very long for *if* you lived like a Christian in
every area and activity of your life. At the same
time we were holding the line on sex and steeling
ourselves to die for the faith if need be, we were
failing to *live* the faith in all sorts of other occasions that were presented to us every day.

I don't think this was the fault of our teachers so
much as it was of the Christian community in general. People don't really learn the values of a society, or of a community, through words. They learn
through observing what *other people do*. That,
they know, is the real interpretation of the words.
Saint Ignatius of Loyola is credited with having
said, "In the eyes of God our words have only the
value of our actions." If this is true of God, it is
also true of man. We believe what people do, not
what they say.

If the Christian community *in fact* makes its peace
with the world, then Christians grow up believing
that the world and Christianity are friends. So we
grew up as Catholics believing that the contempo-
rary American way of life was our ally. We just

didn't have before our eyes the example of any Christian who took a stand against society, except in the areas I have already mentioned.

Insofar as the ordinary morality of the Ten Commandments was concerned, society was, theoretically at least, on the side of Christianity. What society had no scruples about did not trouble our consciences either. Ordinary morality for us dealt with the issues ordinary people were concerned about. After all, the ordinary person was supposed to be Christian. Overt lying, stealing, killing, etc. were wrong because society condemned them. And because society condemned them so strongly, the finer ways of doing these same things, which society had devised and accepted, were not even present to our minds as moral issues. Manipulative advertising, deceptive packaging, phony food products, inflated prices, industrial pollution, "big stick" diplomacy, aid to military dictatorships— these were just what "business" or "politics" meant.

We knew racial segregation was wrong. But since every white Christian we knew went along with the system, it never occurred to us it was anything a Christian should take a stand on. We knew poverty was an evil. But since all the Christians we knew set their own life-style pretty much as if the poor did not exist, we thought Christian concern for the poor just meant giving clothes and money and donating some of your time to charitable works of mercy. It never entered our minds to take a stand against those political, economic or social structures of society that were universally accepted—

or seemed to be—by every believing Christian we knew.

To some extent the same picture is true today. We can hardly expect high school students to believe that Christianity requires them to break with their subculture when they see no evidence that their parents have in any way broken with the prevailing attitudes and values of American culture. If the adults are doing pretty much what all the other adults do, we can expect the kids to do pretty much what all the other kids do. The spirituality of martyrdom is taught by actions, not by words.

Examples in Our Day

But there are examples of people who have taken courageous stands:

• We have seen large numbers of Christians—and non-Christians as well—go to prison rather than take part in what they considered an immoral war.

• A Doctor Kelly in Chicago took his family into voluntary exile in Ireland rather than pay taxes which would be used to procure government-financed abortions.

• In 1974 over 50,000 persons refused to pay the federal excise tax on phone bills, levied to pay for war costs.

• At one southern university several professors lost their jobs a few years ago because of their stand in favor of racial integration. Others have been assassinated or beaten up in demonstration marches for the same cause.

• And as I write this, women and men in Northern Ireland are risking death and retaliation from both sides by marching for peace in the Catholic-Protestant conflict there.

• In another form of persecution, Ralph Nader was the victim of a muckraking investigation of his private life after his exposure of the automobile industry's neglect of human safety. Nader sued General Motors for invasion of privacy and won a $25,000 settlement out of court. Had they succeeded in turning up any scandal in his life, or had Nader been less able to defend himself in the law courts, he would have had to suffer for taking on the Goliath of American industry.

The significant thing about all these examples is that every one of them involves the *initiative of laypersons*. Not one case we have mentioned expresses an official Church decision. The values involved are Christian. But the particular judgment in each case is that of an individual. This is as it should be.

Whether a particular war is or is not unjust; whether one should go as far as voluntary exile rather than contribute tax money to abortions; whether a peace march under a concrete set of circumstances is worth the threat of death: these are questions the Church does not—and normally could not—answer. To make a correct judgment about the concrete reality of matters like these is seldom easy, and to do it one should, as a general rule, be *secular*—that is, involved in, close to, a part of, the reality one is called upon to judge.

The man who is personally subject to the draft is the one to whom, ultimately, we should expect God to give the grace to know whether he should or should not go. The Church's teachings can guide him; a good confessor or spiritual director can help him discern the movements and motivations of his heart. But no one can make his decision for him. That is his responsibility, and as a Christian he should accept it.

Vatican II teaches: "Laymen should also know that it is generally the function of their well-formed Christian conscience to see that the divine law is inscribed in the life of the earthly city. . . . Let the layman not imagine that his pastors are always. . . [ready to] give him a concrete solution, or even that such is their mission. Rather, enlightened by Christian wisdom and giving close attention to the teaching authority of the Church, let the layman take on his distinctive role" (*Pastoral Constitution on the Church in the Modern World*, 43).

What this "distinctive role" is, the Council makes very clear: "The laity must take on the renewal of the temporal order as their own special obligation. Led by the light of the gospel and the mind of the Church, and motivated by Christian love, let them act directly and definitively in the temporal sphere. As citizens they must cooperate with other citizens, using their own particular skills and acting on their own responsibility (*Decree on the Apostolate of the Laity*, 7).

In other words, every Christian is called to be a *prophet*. The prophet is a person who speaks the

Word of God *in a context*. He or she doesn't just *preach* God's Word; but *applies* it, with wisdom given from above, to the concrete reality of a particular situation.

The Spirit of Your Father

To be a Christian *in the world*, a lay Christian, is to be a prophet in the home and in the marketplace; to bear witness by action in all of the affairs of men. And this requires both fortitude and prudence.

The lay Christian is called upon to take a stand on gospel values in the midst of the very complex, ambiguous situations in this seldom black-and-white world out of which "the very web of his existence is woven." To live, and respond as a Christian, in the "ordinary circumstances of family and social life, in each and all of the secular professions and occupations" requires men and women who are as resourceful as serpents and as straightforward as doves (see Mt 10:16).

Jesus himself acknowledged this complexity. He did not lay down for us any rigid rules to follow beyond the general guiding principles of Christian morality. He provided no detailed instructions, because detailed instructions are not possible when we are talking about a Christian response to all the changing, multitudinous, evolving, interwoven moral problems of family, social and economic life. Jesus even told us not to be too concerned ahead of time about what we are to say or do when called upon to bear witness to him in the world. "When the hour comes, you will be given what you are to say. You yourselves will not be the speakers; the Spirit of your Father will be speaking in you" (Mt 10:19-20).

This doesn't mean we needn't *prepare* for that hour. For the Spirit to speak in us when the time comes presupposes that we are men and women of prayer.

Our time, our "hour," is every moment in life when we have to make a moral decision about how to apply the gospel to the concrete reality of our situation—at home, at work, at play, or in the exercise of our civic responsibility. If we don't have the habit of *pondering God's Word* in our hearts, we will never know how to apply it in our lives.

If we do not reflect on the things that go on within and around us—as Mary "treasured all these things and reflected on them in her heart" (Lk 2:19)—we will never *grow* to the level of Christian prudence we need. Good judgment is learned by trial and error. And that is why lay people have to be willing to make their own decisions about how to apply the gospel to their lives—and to their world. They must let God teach them through their successes and through their mistakes.

Freedom From Fear

There is something else we need in order to really see clearly what we ought to do in a particular situation: We need to be *interiorly free*.

To be free in this world presupposes that we have, in a deep and radical way, in the roots of our heart, "renounced" this world for the sake of the Kingdom of God. Even though we are dealt into society's game, and have not withdrawn our stakes from this world, we have not really invested all that we are in what happens to us here and now. Our real treasure must be in heaven.

This leaves us free to play boldly and coolly by Christ's principles, because we are not paralyzed by a life-and-death concern over losing any particular pot. We have already bought the field in which our treasure, and that of those whom we love, is safely hidden. All that concerns us now is how to bear the most effective witness to Christ during our stay in this world, and how we can best contribute to the good of our fellow men by building up the Kingdom of God in love.

Fear is our greatest obstacle. And the only ultimate answer to fear is to embrace everything we are afraid of. Christians must embrace the cross; we must see martyrdom as our fulfillment, not our diminishment. We must be people who, fundamentally, deeply, are crucified to this world and to whom the world is crucified (see Gal 6:14). Our hopes must be secure in God.

To overcome fear is our daily struggle. The spirituality of martyrdom is a constant victory over fear, but it is victory through struggle. The real temptation of the secular Christian is not just to "sin" in the ways that society understands—to murder, steal, commit adultery as the culture itself defines these words. It is rather to go along with what the culture approves of without asking too many questions. To kill when society says it is legitimate or even one's civic duty; to steal by implementing company policies that are perfectly legal and terribly immoral; to hide one's light under a basket and not be a sign in the midst of "an evil, faithless age" (Mt 16:4)—these are the sins that destroy us.

The Christian temptation is to turn down the light of the gospel until its rays don't reach very far beyond the intimate circle of one's own, personal space. We do this because we are afraid of martyrdom, afraid to come into open conflict with the forces of sin in our culture.

We are afraid because we know in our hearts that Christians in conflict with the powers of evil only win by losing. We win the moral victory, but we lose the physical fight. The price we pay for the integrity of our souls—of our personhood, our conscience, our interior freedom—is the dissolution of our lives on this earth. We see our possessions divided among our enemies, our circle of friends dissolved, our hopes for the future shattered. Like Christ, our "hour" of victory is the hour of our defeat.

We understand martyrdom as a way of life when we recognize that the spirituality of martyrdom is something that belongs *inseparably* to the state of Christian secularity, to the condition of lay Christians living and bearing witness in this world. Lay people are witnesses, because that is what it means to be a Christian. They are martyrs, because you cannot bear witness *in* this world, as a part of secular society, without coming into conflict with the world. And the person who comes into conflict with this world as a witness to Jesus Christ will pay the price.

To accept this risk; to live boldly with the account mounting up, knowing that sooner or later the world is going to exact its price in retaliation—this is the spirituality of martyrdom, the spirituality of Christian risk.

Prophet, Priest and King

The basic premise of Christianity is that the gospel is *news* to this world. The Good News is news. To be news, it has to be new—new as Jesus Christ was new and will always be new, "the same yesterday, today, and forever" (Heb 13:8-9).

But what is new is different; and what is different provokes opposition. And so Christians expect to find themselves, as a matter of course, in a more or less constant state of being opposed: opposed *to* and opposed *by* the predominate forces that set the course of this world.

It is not that the Christian sets out to be different, as if there were a value in that. Nonconformity as such is not a Christian ideal; and a critical, or negative attitude toward the world is certainly not a Christian trait. But the Christian realizes that as the world rises toward God, God's truth is *always* becoming more visible to the alert, believing heart as something just a little bit different, and a little bit better, than anything the world has guessed at up till now.

The truth of God is "ever ancient, ever new." And every man instructed in the Kingdom of God, Jesus said, is like the head of a household who is constantly drawing out of his storeroom "both the new and the old" (Mt 13:52). This is why the Church is the most conservative, as well as the most prophetic, of all human institutions: She never stops believing anything she received from the beginning, and she never accepts as final any level of human understanding about the truth and values of God.

If we translate this down to practical terms, on the level of each person's day-to-day existence, this means that no Christian should expect to be able to live a "normal" life according to the established patterns of society. What is "normal" in any society is already something Christianity must be challenging, something the Christian is required to go beyond. What is "normal" for the Christian is to be a prophet to his or her own age.

Sometimes this is a matter of standing *against* society. But frequently the Christian's stand will not be so much against what society sees and accepts, but simply *beyond* it. Even in the best of cultures or civilizations, the "world" plays by its own rules. And these rules, even when they are not "bad" or positively hostile to Christian values, are nevertheless inclined to bypass them or ignore them.

Most people choose their jobs, for example, with the idea of making a living for themselves, hopefully by doing something they like to do. They marry someone with whom they think they will be happy, and look forward to the fulfillment of raising a family. They find friends with whom they get along, whose company they enjoy, and spend pleasant times with them. All this is good, very good. There is nothing bad or anti-Christian about any of it. We could recite the whole litany of human occupations, and after each we could echo the words of Genesis: "God said, 'Let it be!' . . . And God saw that it was good."

But there is something more. Christ came to transform all of human life, every element and area of human existence. There is no human interest or occupation that the gospel leaves untouched. This is why the witness of Christians in the world is not just to protest against what is evil and stand against it, but to *transform what is good* and take it beyond itself. This is the priesthood of the faithful: to consecrate the world, lift it up, offer it to God as creation redeemed and reestablished in Jesus Christ (see Colossians).

The Christian is anointed at Baptism, not only to be a prophet, but also to be a priest and king. As priest, our task is to lift up this world to the transforming power of grace. As king, or partaker in the kingship of Christ, we are in this world not just "to cultivate and care for it" (Gn 2:15), but to take responsibility for its *renovation* as a steward of the Kingdom of God.

Jesus said, "See, I make all things new!" (Rv 21:5). And every baptized Christian is assigned to that great work. To each has been given the Holy Spirit—and gifts that flow from the Spirit—so as to be able to work until the Master returns. Our task is not only to avoid sin but to bear fruit in the vineyard of the Lord. We are not to bury our talent in the ground for safekeeping, but to risk it for the up-building of the Kingdom of God. The Christian's purpose on earth is to be the light of the world, the salt of the earth, the leaven working in the dough until all the bread of this world rises as a pure offering to God.

The person who accepts this task cannot expect to "fit in." It is not so much that the world is *opposed* to its own transformation by grace. Business life, family life, social life: all these have nothing to lose, really, and everything to gain by being bathed in the light of the gospel and oriented toward the Kingdom of God. There is no other way they can realize their own potential. But this does not mean the world will not *resist* this transformation. There is an inertia in the affairs of men. No matter how much change and evolution our human institutions undergo, they tend to remain in their natural orbit. And their natural orbit revolves around this earth, not around the Kingdom of God.

In business life, it is not the natural, spontaneous thing for men to work as Paul advises: "Whatever you do, work at it with your whole being. Do it for the Lord rather than for men" (Col 3:23). Paul has to complain, even about the Christians, "Everyone is busy seeking his own interests rather than those of Christ Jesus" (Phil 2:21).

The immediate interest of business is profit. Too often it becomes the ultimate interest as well, the first and last consideration that determines every choice. Christians who look not primarily to profit (although without profits they won't be working very long) but to the service they can render to God and neighbor in love may find themselves passing up a lot of opportunities to make more money. If they are working for someone else, they may not fit very well into the company. This is a "martyrdom" situation: by the values Christians accept the risk of losing, they bear witness to a value that transcends this world.

In social life, we admire what Jesus said about giving parties: "Whenever you give a lunch or dinner, do not invite your friends or brothers or relatives or wealthy neighbors. . . . No, . . .invite beggars and the crippled, the lame and the blind" (Lk 14:12-13). But our spontaneous bent in giving a party is not to think of those who are in *need* of our love. We think of people we enjoy. (And this might be the point: to find the deeper joy of relating to people in a new, undreamed-of way).

But if we decided, for example, to go out of our way to include black people in our circle of friends, (or white people, if the reader is black), we would very soon know what it means to be a "martyr" in modern society. It is not that our other friends would necessarily object; they might be grateful for the opportunity to break out of their own cultural backyard. But we wouldn't know till we tried it. We might find ourselves ostracized. The "martyrdom" is in taking the risk.

When it comes to family life, it is impossible to say much in a brief space. Let us just recall the teaching of Pope Paul VI (given in an apostolic exhortation on devotion to the Blessed Mother, April, 1974) that the true, the theological nature of the family is to be a "domestic church"; that is, the Church of Jesus Christ, the People of God, made present and realized on the level of the home. The family cannot be this, explains Pope Paul, unless it is a worshiping community, unless the family *prays together*.

This is not something families spontaneously do in our culture. And there are many other ways in which the style of life in Christian families is determined, not by the values of the gospel, but by the trends and currents—even by the fads and follies—of modern society, good and bad. Praying together would be a start at reversing this.

Pope Paul recognizes the difficulty—the apparent impossibility, even—of getting families together for anything these days, and especially for family prayer. But the words in which he asks us to try are an echo of what we have been presenting here as the spirit of Christian martyrdom: "When it comes to the style of life he is going to lead, it is characteristic of the Christian not to give in to circumstances, but to overcome them; not to just give up, but to make an effort."

Living as an "Outsider"

The point is that anyone who truly accepts the Gospels, has already become an "outsider" to human society. Of course, in one sense, such a person is more deeply involved in human society, in the unrolling drama of human history, than ever before. In the committed Christian the Incarnation of Christ, the enfleshed presence of God to the world, is continued. But at the same time a Christian is under the world's sentence of death: The place the world would consign him or her is "outside the walls," on the hill of crucifixion.

Christians should not need, like Patty Hearst, to have the Symbionese Liberation Army break into their apartments and challenge them to a radical way of life. They already have the Good News that is the only true hope of the world, and they have staked their whole life on that hope. From the position of disciples of Jesus Christ they have taken a stance toward life and its values that revolutionizes everything they know and jeopardizes everything they have: everything they own; every friendship not rooted in Christ; every expectation of a "normal," peaceful life in this world secured at the cost of "fitting in" to society's norms.

They are as much "outlaws" in society's eyes as any revolutionary ever was. But not because they break the law or put themselves outside of society's law. It is because they have accepted the law of Christ which is unacceptable to many of the ruling forces of this world. Christians have broken *out* of the law of this world to live by a higher, more demanding law. And those who go *beyond* the level of ideals prescribed by the law are less acceptable to the men and women of this world than those who just fail to live up to them.

No one likes to be low man on the totem pole. Those whose ideals seem to place them above others are more threatening to society's sense of security than the criminal whom society can look down upon. The world can make peace with its prodigals; the prophets must be stoned. Between Christ and Barabbas we have seen society choose.

There was a time when the break between Christianity and our culture was not as clear and open as it is today. There was a time when we didn't feel our Christianity challenged at every turn in life, and for that very reason we were less apt to see the challenge where it really existed. But the flags are flying now.

There is no effort now to disguise the value system of our culture. The Watergate conspirators were frank. The military are non-apologetic. Business men are hard. Youth is unblushing. War is ruthless; abortions are legal; pornography is everywhere; business is amoral; sex is taken for granted; drugs are commonplace; politics is venal. The Christian wrappings are off; it's a pagan society.

A Truly "Lay" Spirituality

Christians accept the fact that Christ's truth and goodness are unacceptable to this world. But they do not accept the fact that they *must be*. They are willing to accept a life of suffering and rejection by this world, in company with Christ crucified and rejected, but they are *not willing to condemn the world as unchangeable*.

This is the difference between the Christian and the political revolutionary. Revolutions are based on despair—despair of the other side's ability to convert. Revolutionaries will destroy what they cannot change. They will kill those they cannot win over.

But Christians are sent to save not to destroy. They believe the world can be redeemed—has been redeemed, is being redeemed, will be redeemed. Christ has conquered; Jesus is Lord. And his followers bear witness in the world conscious that the victory has already been won. It simply has to be extended to all who are willing to receive it.

St. Paul held up as a model to Christians a life of loving witness in the midst of insult and rejection. What we should notice here is that the emphasis is on *love* and on *hope*, not on the attitude of the world itself: "We have become a spectacle to the universe, to angels and men alike. We are fools on Christ's account. . . .We are the weak ones. . . .They sneer at us. . . .When we are insulted we respond with a blessing. Persecution comes our way; we bear it patiently. We are slandered, and we try conciliation. We have become the world's refuse, the scum of all; that is the present state of affairs" (1 Cor 4:9-10, 12-13).

That is, paradoxically, *always* the present state of affairs and *only* the present state of affairs! Things are always bad, but always getting better. There is always persecution going on, and always conversion taking place. Christ is being crucified, and rising again daily in new and multiplied life.

Christians who accept to be the mystery of the Incarnation in this world give Christ flesh in the City of Man—in family life, social life, business and professional life, political life—by offering their body and blood to be the Body of Christ today. These Christians will experience the paschal mystery in their lives, the mystery of Christ's dying and rising in simultaneous defeat and victory.

This is a time when Christians need one another. And the world, whether it knows it or not, has need of us as never before. The home and the marketplace, business, politics, professional and social life: all need prophets, priests and stewards of the kingship of Christ.

The point of lay spirituality is not to see how close lay people can come to living the life of a monk or a nun in their spare time. Nor should it try to adapt the spirituality of the great religious orders to lay needs and to encourage lay people to see their apostolate as helping the priests or sisters in their work. Not that there is anything wrong with this: Third Orders and religious organizations of laity can only add vitality to the lay person's spiritual life. But the *substance* of lay spirituality does not lie here. It exists in the challenges of living as a witness and disciple of Jesus the Lord in the midst of *secular* life.

Lay people have to learn to surf; not to look for the tranquil waters of some restful, spiritual retreat in order to tend to their "spiritual life." Their spiritual life is where the waves are; if they want to get anywhere, they must learn to ride them.

It is the ups and down of married life, professional life, civic life that will carry them forward if they learn to be surfers. And then, if they have the stomach for it, the higher the waves are, the faster the waves will take them to the shore.

In Solitary Witness

We have been stressing all along the need for Christian community in our lives. That need is real. Without the support of our fellow believers we won't go very far, and we won't last very long. We must build community.

We *must* build community, but we *must not* wait for it.

Christian community is built—can only be built— by those who are willing to walk alone, who have tried to walk alone, who know what it is to walk alone. A Christian community is a community of Abrahams: of people who have "left country, kinsfolk, and their father's house" to follow the voice of God into the wilderness, wherever it might lead.

We need the support of others, but we cannot make it a *condition* for following Christ ourselves—in solitary witness, if need be.

There is a man of our times—a saint of our times, I believe—who rose to this challenge. He was an Austrian farmer, a young man with a wife and two small children, called up for service in the German army under Hitler in February, 1943. His name was Franz Jaeggerstaetter.

Jaeggerstaetter did not believe in Hitler. He thought he was an immoral man. He thought Hitler's government was an immoral government; his war an immoral war.

He was the only man in his village to vote against Austria's union with Nazi Germany.

When hail destroyed the crops in his area, his crops included, and the German government provided disaster relief, he would not accept the money.

When he was called to serve in the army, he felt he could not in conscience agree to serve.

So he went to his parish priest. "Is it moral for me to serve in the German army?" he asked. The priest assured him that it was. He went to another priest, in a village down the road. This priest suspected he was a Gestapo agent, but he too assured Franz he could serve in the German army. Finally he went to the bishop. The bishop too encouraged him to serve in Hitler's army.

Jaeggerstaetter then reported to the induction center and told them he could not in conscience serve in the German army.

The military did their best for him. They didn't want this poor young farmer to be beheaded, which was the penalty for refusal to serve in the army. They got him a lawyer, they offered him a place in the medical corps where he would not have to kill anyone.

But Jaeggerstaetter's difficulty was with service in Hitler's army as such. Hitler was immoral, the government was immoral, the war was immoral; he wanted nothing to do with any of it.

"If I went into the medical corps and wore the uniform, I would be pretending to agree with Hitler's government, with the war. It would be a lie."

"Franz," his lawyer asked him, "has any German or Austrian bishop, in a pastoral letter, a sermon, or anything else, called upon Catholics not to support the war or to refuse military service?"

"Not that I know of," he responded.

"And there are millions of other German Catholics who don't have any problem in their conscience about it. Why is it you have a problem?"

"I guess they don't have the grace to see it," was all that he could say. "But I do have the grace to see it, so I can't serve in the army."

Franz Jaeggerstaetter was executed on August 9, 1943—in solitary witness.[1]

None of us today would even argue the point whether Hitler's war was immoral. But would a Catholic in similar circumstances today do what Jaeggerstaetter did? Or would he serve in another Hitler's army?

Let me rearrange the problem just a little.

Suppose you are a plumber in Munich, Germany, during World War II. One day the government asks

1. See Gordon Zahn, *In Solitary Witness,* Beacon Press, 1968, p. 57-58, 86.

you to go to a little village outside of Munich to install some showers in a government camp. The name of the village is Dachau.

You begin setting up the showers, then you ask the government representative, "Where is the water supply we're going to hook up to?"

"Oh," he replies, "I'll let you in on a little secret. These aren't going to be real showers—exactly. This is supposed to be a concentration camp, you know. We don't hook up to a water supply but to those cyanide gas tanks over there. We tell the prisoners they are taking showers. They strip down and go peacefully into that big concrete room where the spigots are. Then we lock the doors and turn on the gas. It's the most convenient way to do it."

At this point you begin to get some second thoughts about the job. "I don't know if I want to do this job," you say. "I didn't know I was building an execution chamber to kill Jews."

"Well," he says, "you're a nice guy. I'll give you some advice. If you don't install the showers, someone else will. It doesn't make a lot of difference who we get. But if I have to tell the government that you refused to do it, you will be the first one into the showers!

"So why don't you think it over for awhile. Go home and talk to your parish priest. And come back and see me tomorrow."

You go home and you talk to the priest. Do you know what he would have told you?

There is a classical moral distinction between "formal evil," which means doing something bad yourself, and "material cooperation with evil," which means helping someone else do it. To shoot someone is formal evil. To sell a man a gun, knowing he is going to shoot someone, that is material cooperation.

Now the moralists used to say that material cooperation with evil is *not* wrong, given three conditions:

1) You don't do, or desire to do, anything yourself that is actually evil.

2) You can't stop the evil from being done by refusing to cooperate.

3) You will suffer a proportionately great evil yourself if you don't cooperate.

The priest would probably have told you, "Look, you are not being asked to do anything that is a sin yourself. You are not killing anybody; you don't want to kill anybody. You are just putting in pipes. If you don't put them in, they'll get somebody else. And they'll kill you if you don't. Go ahead and put them in.

"And while you are doing it, pray for the people who are going to die there."

So you probably would have put in the pipes. That's what all the other Catholics in Germany under Hitler did. And the Protestants too—the whole Christian population. There were a large number of exceptions, like Franz Jaeggerstaetter and Dietrich Bonhoeffer and Blessed Maximilian

Kolbe, the priest from Poland who volunteered to die in place of a married man condemned to the starvation bunker at Auschwitz. But the thousands of Christians who were imprisoned for opposition to Hitler's regime are still only a handful among the millions of people, most of them Christians in name, who made up the population of Germany under Hitler.

Hitler was able to plunge most of the Western Hemisphere into war and kill an estimated six million Jews in cold blood because of the principle of "material cooperation"!

Witness—the Only Choice

Suppose everyone who disapproved of Hitler's government, his methods, his war had just stopped—cold. No work, no taxes, no military service, no movement, nothing! It would have been impossible to kill them all. There never would have been a war.

I'm not talking here about organized resistance: political parties, underground networks and the like. The Gestapo had a pretty good record for keeping such things from getting started. I am talking about what Franz Jaeggerstaetter did: 30 million acts of individual, isolated, solitary refusal to cooperate. Thirty million Christians who, in the privacy of their own consciences, without knowing whether anyone else would support or second them, would just refuse to cooperate.

It would have been *effective*, but that is not the real point.

We already understand an argument based on *effectiveness*—on *political power*. The picture is appealing because there is *power* in 30 million individuals who are willing to die one by one rather than cooperate with evil.

But political power and martyrdom are not the same thing. I am all for Christians using political power. In fact, we are obliged to use all the legitimate political means at our disposal to bring about a reform of society. This is a major element in the lay apostolate. But we already understand the use of power. I want to call our attention to something else, something we are not sufficiently aware of.

Jesus did not send us first and foremost to change social structures through the use of political power. I am sure he wants us to do this. But what the gospels speak about is *witness*: and the Greek word for a witness is *martyr*.

Early Christians were called martyrs because *they bore witness* to what they believed in. They died for it. They were not canonized because they accomplished anything, or even asked whether they would accomplish anything. They were not trying to bring about the fall of Rome by demonstrating against it with their blood. They were just refusing to cooperate with evil, bearing witness to Christ, and paying the price for it.

"Whoever would preserve his life will lose it, but whoever loses his life for my sake and the gospel's will preserve it" (Mk 8:35).

What Christianity is all about is witness. It is the only real duty we have here on earth: to bear witness to Christ. It is the only thing Jesus himself ever did: express the love of God for men; express his own love, in the name of all men, to the Father. In the Book of Revelation he is called "the Witness. . . Faithful and True" (Rv 3:14; 19:11).

The man who dies expressing what he stands for has achieved the purpose of life—if what he stands for is the truth of Jesus Christ. To live as a martyr—as a witness who constantly risks and is willing to lose everything he has, including life itself—should be the normal condition for Christians.

We can only keep what we have for a limited number of years. But what we lose for Christ is ours forever. Witness—not success, or even survival—is what we're all about.

A Christian has no choice about some things. The gospel tells us we cannot follow Jesus Christ unless we renounce everything else in this world, including life itself. We are not offered the option of carrying the cross or not. "If a man wishes to come after me, he must deny his very self, take up his cross, and follow in my steps" (Mk 8:34). Our only option is the *way* we choose to be crucified:
  —by staying in the world and *risking* everything we have;
  —by leaving the world and *renouncing* everything we have.

Religious life is a way of deliberate, voluntary renunciation. Lay life is a way of constant, deliberately-incurred risk. Religious bear witness to their faith by renouncing things directly and in *fact*. They renounce them *effectively*; they get rid of them.

Lay persons bear witness by renouncing things indirectly through their *acts*. They renounce them *affectively* in their hearts by living the gospel so uncompromisingly in this world that they risk having everything taken away from them.

It's just two sides of the same cross, if you will. And the monk and the martyr are both hanging in there together.

We lost sight of lay spirituality when we accepted the principle that it was possible to be a good Christian and live a normal life in this world. It is not. But the alternative is not to *leave* the world, *give up* social, family and professional life, and be a monk. That is *one* alternative, and a perfectly valid one. It is religious spirituality. But the other alternative is to *stay in* the world and *risk*—to be a martyr.

After all, there's not really anything to worry about. As the two men said on the gallows, "The Lord hasn't let us down yet!"

So you're a plumber today, not in Nazi Germany, but in the United States. You also are called out on a job to put in some pipes. In the process you ask the boss, "Hey, what are we building?"

It's an abortion clinic.

You have a problem in conscience. You don't believe in abortion. Suppose you were to say to your boss that you'd rather not work on that job.

"Look," he says, "you're free to do what you want. But jobs are scarce right now and there's plenty of guys out of work. I can't afford to have a man working for me if I don't know when he's going to work and when he isn't. If you want to quit, quit. But if you don't work on this job, don't come back."

So what do you do?

Well, don't panic. As they said to the man on the gallows, "You haven't got far to go now!"

Take One Step to Begin With

EPILOGUE: *There Goes That Man Again*

I hope this book hasn't struck you like John the Baptist—a voice crying in the desert, "There goes the Lamb of God," but when he passes by, nobody moves.

And then, on the other hand, I hope there has been something of John the Baptist in it: enough to leave you just a little bit stunned, anyway.

I hope the book has upset you.

A religious exhortation is not really valid unless it comforts the afflicted and afflicts the comfortable. If you are afflicted because the Good News has never really seemed to be news, I hope this book is a comfort. And if you are comfortable with your own level of giving and response to the Lord, I hope you now stand afflicted.

Because affliction can lead to conversion. And conversion leads to the Lord.

I have lots of chapters I would like to write yet: on obstacles to response, before and after we believe in the Lord; on the *trust* we can have in the Lord if we risk the way of martyrdom (notice what follows all the challenging passages in the Sermon on the Mount; see Mt 6:25-34); on man's judgment after death as based not on the "sins" he has committed, but on the *fruit* he has or has not borne; on the illusions of beginners in the spiritual life, and the illusions of the more advanced. But these will wait on the Lord's time. There is a lot of road in the spiritual life, and this book aims at no more than to start you off on it.

But has it done that?

What I am most afraid of is that, in spite of my efforts to make everything sound very easy, very simple—three simple steps to personal encounter with Jesus Christ: prayer, conversion and community—you still might feel overwhelmed.

Maybe the examples of conversion of life—Patty Hearst and her radical decision to join the SLA—made you feel you were faced with too big a leap. Maybe the application of Christian principles to the problems of society seems too vast and complicated for you to tackle. Maybe martyrdom sounds like a pretty tough deal.

Well, remember, you are not being asked to start there.

All you are asked to do at this point is *take a first step*.

This is all any faith response can be at the beginning. God doesn't give maps. He goes before you. He goes with you: a cloud by day, a pillar of fire by night. He wants you, like Abraham, like the Wise Men following the star, like John and Andrew starting off behind Jesus at the Jordan, to take a first step toward him and be willing to follow wherever he will lead.

If you don't know where you are going, you will have to keep your eyes on him. It's the only way to travel his road.

I do not want to give the impression in this book that I am suggesting any concrete action at all in the area of personal or societal conversion of life. I haven't presumed to suggest, I hope, how you should eat, drink, dress, drive, work, play or choose your partners at bridge. I haven't offered any program for the reformation of society. I may have emphasized some values and revealed some of my own. But I haven't tried to sell you any concrete choices. Except one: to read and pray over the Scriptures.

The reason: *Only God knows exactly what you should do!*

One of my favorite stories in the Gospels is the story of that woman who kept crying behind Jesus

to come expel a demon from her daughter. She was
a Canaanite—a pagan, not a Jew. And Jesus ignored
her.

He ignored her so long, and she was making such a
din, that even the disciples began to beg him to
give her what she asked for and send her away. Our
Lord responded with what sounds like the rudest
answer in the New Testament: "It is not right to
take the food of sons and daughters and throw it
to the dogs" (Mt 15:26).

But he knew the woman he was dealing with. She
must have had a very strong self-image. Undaunted,
she came back with: "Please, Lord, . . .even the
dogs eat the leavings that fall from their masters'
tables" (Mt 15:27).

And he cured her daughter: "Woman, you have
great faith! Your wish will come to pass" (Mt 15:28;
see also Mk 7:24ff).

Do you see what Jesus did? In a very indirect way
he led her to make an act of faith in the true, the
Jewish religion. When Jesus referred to the "food
of the sons and daughters" she could have taken
this as a cultural comparison and come back with,
"A Canaanite is as good as a Jew any day!" But she
didn't. She took it as a reference to the fact God
has chosen the Jews, whatever their cultural level
might be, and made them his Chosen People. They
had the true word, the true revelation from God.
And she conceded this.

This act of faith was all Jesus asked of her. He
didn't follow up with what, to us, would be the
logical conclusion: "Join the Jewish religion; be-

come a Jew." There were too many cultural blocks in the way. Besides, the moment was coming when God's revelation would not be tied to an ethnic people but preached to the world at large. The light was about to be given to the Gentiles. He left her with what she could respond to at the time.

And that is what he does with us. God knows how to "temper the wind to the shorn lamb." He never asks more than we can give at the moment.

Don't ask of yourself more than the Lord asks. John Woolman had the grace to adopt this attitude toward those he was trying to convert; we should show the same graciousness to ourselves: "I found by experience that to *keep pace* with the gentle actions of Truth, and *never more but as that opens the way*, is necessary for the true servants of Christ" (*The Journal of John Woolman*, emphases added).

So begin with prayer. Begin by reading the Scripture and reflecting on it until you come to some decisions that change your life in some way. How great or small a way is not the issue. Just change. And Christ will make the next move.

Take a first step. There is no telling where it may lead you.

And now the ball is in your court. Have courage and trust in the Lord. Martyrdom isn't really so bad after all, they tell me, once you get used to it.

As the lynch mob said when they rode away, "Just hang in there till the Lord comes!"

And keep swinging.